High Scorer's Choice Series

IELTS 5 Practice Tests

Academic Set 3

(Tests No. 11-15)

High Scorer's Choice Series, Book 5
IELTS 5 Practice Tests, Academic Set 3 (Tests No. 11–15)
ISBN 9780648000020
Copyright © 2017 Simone Braverman, Robert Nicholson.
First Edition May 2017

Available in print and digital formats
Accompanying audio recordings to be downloaded on the following webpage:
http://www.ielts-blog.com/ielts-practice-tests-downloads/

IELTS® is a registered trademark of University of Cambridge ESOL, the British Council, and IDP Education Australia, which neither sponsor nor endorse this book.

To contact the authors:
Email: simone@ielts-blog.com
Website: www.ielts-blog.com

Acknowledgements

The authors hereby acknowledge the following websites for their contributions to this book (see the webpage below for a complete list):

www.ielts-blog.com/acknowledgements/

While every effort has been made to contact copyright holders it has not been possible to identify all sources of the material used. The authors and publisher would in such instances welcome information from copyright holders to rectify any errors or omissions

Praise for
High Scorer's Choice Practice Tests

"I am a teacher from Australia. I had a Chinese friend who is studying for the exam and I used these [tests] to help him. I think the papers are very professional and useful. Many of the commercial practice papers are not culturally sensitive but this was not a problem with your tests."
  - *Margaretta from Australia*

"I found out that your practice papers are excellent. I took my IELTS on March 11th and got an Overall Band 8 with listening – 8, reading – 9, writing – 7 and speaking – 7. I spent one month on preparation."
  - *Dr Yadana from London, UK*

"I must tell you that the sample tests I have purchased from you have been the key to my preparation for the IELTS. Being employed full time I do not have the time to attend classes. I downloaded the material and made myself practice a few hours every 2 or 3 days for 3 weeks and was successful on my first trial. I was able to get an average of 7.5 and I was aiming at 7."
  - *Oswaldo from Venezuela*

Finished *one* book? There's more!

High Scorer's Choice - The Complete Series:

Book 1
IELTS 5 Practice Tests, Academic Set 1 (Tests No. 1–5)

Book 2
IELTS 5 Practice Tests, General Set 1 (Tests No. 1–5)

Book 3
IELTS 5 Practice Tests, Academic Set 2 (Tests No. 6–10)

Book 4
IELTS 5 Practice Tests, General Set 2 (Tests No. 6–10)

Book 5
IELTS 5 Practice Tests, Academic Set 3 (Tests No. 11–15)

Book 6
IELTS 5 Practice Tests, General Set 3 (Tests No. 11–15)

CONTENTS

Download Audio Content

In order to download the audio content please use a desktop computer (not a mobile device) with a reliable internet connection and open the following webpage in your browser:

http://www.ielts-blog.com/ielts-practice-tests-downloads/

Follow instructions on the webpage to save all audio files on your computer. The files are in mp3 format and you will need an audio player to listen to them (any modern computer has that type of software preinstalled).

How to prepare for IELTS

There are two ways for you to use these practice tests for your exam preparation. You can either use them to work on your technique and strategy for each IELTS skill, or you can use them to simulate a real exam and make sure you will do well under time pressure.

Option 1   Use practice tests to work on your IELTS skills (no time limits)

To prepare well for the IELTS exam you need to have a strategy for each sub-test (Listening, Reading, Writing and Speaking). This means knowing what actions to take, and in which order, when you receive a test paper. If you are working with the IELTS self-study book "Target Band 7 – How to Maximize Your Score", all the necessary tips are located in the book. You need to read and then apply these tips and techniques when you are practicing on some of these tests. Don't time yourself, concentrate on learning the techniques and making sure they work for you.

If you purchased the practice tests in digital format, you will need to print out some pages, for easier learning and to be able to work in the same way as in the real test (on paper). Print the Listening questions and the Reading passages and questions. You can read the Writing and Speaking questions from your computer or mobile device, to save paper and ink. If you have the paperback format, this doesn't apply to you. Use Table of Contents on the previous page to navigate this book.

If Listening is one of your weaker skills, use transcripts while listening to recordings, when you hear words or sentences that you don't understand. Stop the recording, rewind, locate in the transcript the sentence you had a problem with, read it, and then listen to the recording again.

If Reading is hard for you, after doing the Reading test use the Reading Answer Help section of these practice tests to understand why the answers in the Answer key are correct. It will show you the exact locations of the answers in the Reading passages.

To compare your own writing to high-scoring samples go to Example Writing Answers and read them. Note the way the information is selected and reported in Writing Task 1, and the way an essay is organised in Writing Task 2.

To practice in Speaking, either read to yourself the Speaking test questions or get a friend to help with that. Record your answers and then listen to the recording. Note where you make long pauses while searching for the right word, pay attention to your errors and your pronunciation. Compare your own performance to that of students in sample interviews, and read their Examiner's reports.

Option 2   **Use practice tests to simulate the real test (strict time limits)**

This option will require some prep work before you can start a simulated test. Print out or photocopy the blank Test Answer Sheets for Listening and Reading and prepare some ruled paper on which to write your Writing Task 1 and 2. Also, think of a way to record yourself in the Speaking sub-test. Get a watch, preferably with a timer. Allocate 3 hours of uninterrupted time.

1. Be in a quiet room, put the Listening questions in front of you and start playing the recording. Answer questions as you listen, and write your answers next to the questions in the book.

2. When the recording has finished playing, allocate 10 minutes to transfer all your Listening answers to the Listening Answer Sheet. While you are transferring the answers check for spelling or grammatical errors and if you missed an answer, write your best guess.

3. Put the Reading passages and questions in front of you and set the timer to 60 minutes. Begin reading passages and answering questions. You can write the answers next to the questions or straight on the Answer Sheet. Remember that you don't get extra time to copy answers to the Answer Sheet, and that when 60 minutes are up all your answers must be written on the Answer Sheet.

4. Put the Writing questions in front of you and set the timer to 60 minutes. Make sure you don't use more than 20 minutes for Task 1, including proofreading time, and that you don't use more than 40 minutes for Task 2, with proofreading included.

5. Put the Speaking questions in front of you and begin the interview (remember to record your answers). In Section 2 take the whole 1 minute to prepare your speech and make notes, and then try to speak for 2 minutes (set the timer before you start talking).

6. When you have finished the whole test, take some time to rest, as you may be tired and it may be hard for you to concentrate. Then check your answers in the Listening and Reading against the correct ones in the Answer key, compare your writing tasks to the Example Writing tasks and your recorded speaking to the example interview. Analyse and learn from any mistakes you may find, and especially notice any problems with time management you may have encountered.

    Remember, it is OK to make mistakes while practicing as long as you are learning from them and improving with every test you take.

    Good luck with your exam preparation!

PRACTICE TEST 11

LISTENING

 Download audio recordings for the test here:
http://www.ielts-blog.com/ielts-practice-tests-downloads/

SECTION 1   Questions 1 – 10

Questions 1 – 5

Complete the sentences below.

*Use **NO MORE THAN THREE WORDS AND/OR A NUMBER** from the listening for each answer.*

Example	Answer
Louise needs a bus pass for zones 1 to _____.	*3*

1   Louise's last bus pass began _____ ago.

2   Louise now wants to be contacted by _____.

3   Unlike her previous bus pass, Louise's new one will have a _____ on it.

4   The new bus pass has gone up in price by _____.

5   Louise has to put her _____ on her bus pass to make it valid.

Questions 6 – 8

*Match the bus stops (questions **6 - 8**) with their locations (**A - H**).*

*Write the correct letter (**A - H**) next to questions **6 - 8**.*

BUS STOPS

6   Bus Stop Q   _____

7   Bus Stop G   _____

8   Bus Stop A   _____

LOCATIONS	
A	West Gate Shopping Centre
B	West Howe
C	The University
D	The Town Centre Post Office
E	The Town Hall
F	The Hospital
G	The Arrowdown Sports Centre
H	The Cinema

Questions 9 and 10

*Choose **TWO** letters, **A - E**.*

*Which **TWO** of the following will Louise get discounts on prices with her bus pass?*

A   The cinema

B   Local train services

C   The local football club

D   The local theatre

E   The local museum

SECTION 2   *Questions 11 - 20*

Questions 11 – 15

Answer the questions below.

Use **NO MORE THAN THREE WORDS AND/OR A NUMBER** *from the listening for each answer.*

11   Which organisation founded the adult education centre?

12   How often is the teaching of the adult education centre's teachers assessed?

13   Where can all the lesson resources be found online?

14   How long is one of the teachers' weekly online tutorial sessions?

15   At what time does the administration section in Langdon Street close to the general public?

Questions 16 – 20

Complete the table below on the courses that the Adult Education Centre offers.

*Write **NO MORE THAN THREE WORDS** from the listening for each answer.*

Course	Notes
Languages	* European languages and others. * For different abilities. * **(16)** _____ available on the website.
Business	* Short 1-day courses or longer ones to gain a qualification. * Computer software, **(17)** _____, search engine optimisation and website development. * Most popular courses. * Only 10 people a course so book quickly.
Photography and **(18)** _____	* How to get the most from your camera. * Basic to advanced courses - build up knowledge and learn about your equipment.
Cooking	* Speciality or the popular introduction to cooking. * Basics and some more advanced topics covered. * Learn all about store cupboard ingredients. * Learn important techniques. * **(19)** _____ for fast and fun cooking.
Creative Writing	* Course run by studying practical exercises with discussion and examples. * Gives an insight to the creative process. * Hopeful writers can learn the **(20)** _____ for creating fiction.
Check the website for details of other courses.	

SECTION 3   *Questions 21 – 30*

Questions 21 – 26

Complete the table below on events related to the students' survey mentioned in the listening.

Write **NO MORE THAN TWO WORDS** from the listening for each answer.

Survey on Community Benefits from the Digital Environment		
Topic Number	**Topic**	**Notes**
1	Perceptions of Internet Speed	(**21**) _____, not dial-up
2	Perceptions of Affordability	Avoid questions related to travel to avoid creating (**22**) _____ in the answers
3	Changing Subscriptions and Providers	Focus on locked in contracts and length of (**23**) _____
4	Transparency Regarding (**24**) _____	Very topical; Communication companies look for the best (**25**) _____ from a deal rather than their customers' financial well-being
5	Mobile Phones - users' satisfaction with their (**26**) _____	Topical again; other countries better than this country

Questions 27 and 28

Circle the correct letters **A - C**.

27   When will the four students conduct their survey?

     A   Wednesday afternoon
     B   Friday afternoon
     C   Saturday afternoon

28   Where is the final decision to conduct the survey?

     A   The town centre
     B   The train station
     C   The central shopping mall

Questions 29 and 30

Complete the sentences below.

Use **NO MORE THAN TWO WORDS** *from the listening for each answer.*

29   Abbie suggests that the group meets the next day to collate the survey's results and perform some _____ on them.

30   Martin's trip to the _____ prevents him meeting the others on Sunday evening.

SECTION 4   *Questions 31 – 40*

Questions 31 - 37

Complete the notes below on geothermal energy and Iceland.

Write **NO MORE THAN THREE WORDS AND/OR A NUMBER** *from the listening for each answer.*

Geothermal Energy and Iceland

* Geothermal energy is heat from the Earth
* Found underground; sometimes shallow, sometimes deep (to the magma layer)
* Most of the energy comes from the (**31**) _____ of radioactive minerals (ie: uranium and potassium)

* Iceland at the forefront of geothermal energy for heating and electricity production (currently it supplies 25% of the country's electricity production)
* 84% of energy use is from domestic renewable resources (66% is geothermal)
* In the 20th century, Iceland changed from a poor country to one with a high (**32**) _____

* Iceland is on a geological fault line
* The North American and Eurasian tectonic plates move at (**33**) _____ cm annually
* Creates a lot of volcanic activity and regular (**34**) _____ (not usually dangerous)
* Lots of volcanoes (more than 200) and hot springs
* Approx. 30 volcanoes have erupted since Iceland was populated

* Iceland's geothermal energy comes from 2 types of hot water systems:

1   High Temperature Fields
        Found in the (**35**) _____ or nearby
        Usually at altitude
        The rock is young and permeable
        Groundwater is deep
        Shown at surface usually as (**36**) _____

2   Low Temperature Fields
        Found usually in southwest Iceland
        Shown at surface usually as hot or boiling springs
        Flow rates from almost zero to 180 litres a second
        These fields are thought to be (**37**) _____ (existing a few thousand years)

Page 13

Questions 38 – 40

Complete the diagram below on a geothermal electricity generating plant.

*Write **NO MORE THAN THREE WORDS** from the listening for each answer.*

A Geothermal Electricity Generating Plant

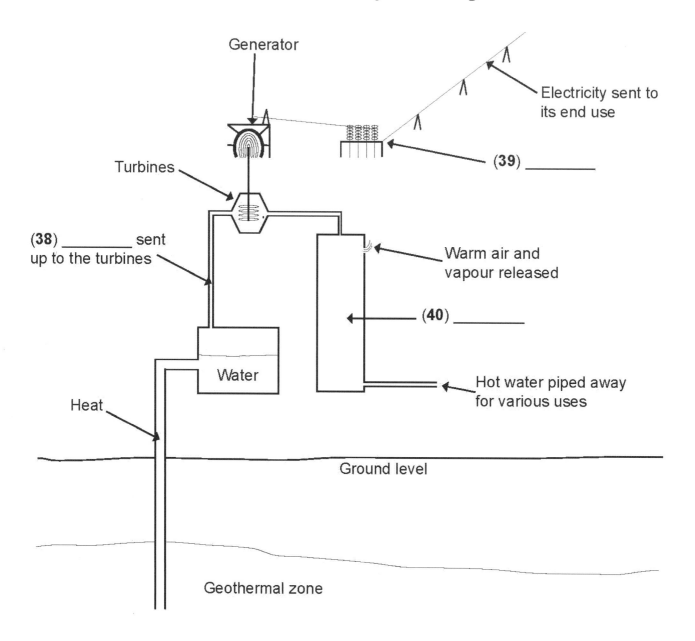

READING

READING PASSAGE 1

*You should spend about 20 minutes on **Questions 1 - 13**, which are based on Reading Passage 1 below.*

Anxiety

Anxiety is a common experience that can be a useful motivator or even lifesaver in situations that are objectively dangerous. However, when the anxiety is out of proportion to the danger inherent in a given situation, is persistent and is markedly disabling, an anxiety disorder can be developed.

Anxiety is an emotion that all people experience from time to time, and we do that for very good reasons. It has been built into us; we have inherited it from our evolutionary past, because, in general, anxiety has a survival function. If there is a real danger for a primitive man, then anxiety kicks in in an adaptive way. We freeze, we stop doing whatever we were doing, we devote all of your attention to the danger, and our bodies react with a big release of adrenalin, an increase in blood flow to the muscles, getting us ready to run as fast as we can or fight as fiercely as we can.

So some anxiety is adaptive, not only for primitive man, but in modern society as well. It helps us to focus on things when we have deadlines and, if someone is driving too fast when we cross the road, it helps us to jump out of the way quickly. So, there is nothing wrong with anxiety in general, and in fact, we would have difficulties if we did not experience it to some extent, but of course it can get problematic if the danger is one that is imagined rather than real, or the danger is something that is exaggerated. In those cases, particularly if the perceived danger is out of proportion to the real danger, and it is persistent and disabling, then there is a danger of an anxiety disorder. About 17 per cent of the population will have an anxiety disorder at some stage in their life.

Anxiety can be caused in a variety of different ways, but any mental disorder is always difficult to diagnose. Scientists are looking at what role genes play in the development of these disorders and are also investigating the effects of environmental factors, such as pollution, physical and psychological stress, and diet. Several parts of the brain are key actors in the production of fear and anxiety. Using brain imaging technology and neurochemical techniques, scientists have discovered that the amygdala plays a significant role in most anxiety disorders. By learning more about how the brain creates fear and anxiety, scientists may be able to devise better treatments for these disorders.

Anxiety disorders are a very costly problem in terms of society. Some published figures show that, in the US, it cost $60 billion in one year in terms of lost productivity and in terms of excessive medical investigations that many people with anxiety seek, often thinking they have a physical problem.

Given all of this, it is rather worrying that anxiety also has a rather low treatment-seeking rate. Only 10 per cent of people with an anxiety disorder will seek treatment. That seems to be largely because people do not realise there are effective treatments available. Most people tend to think they have had it for most of their lives, so it is just their personality and they cannot change their personality, and so they feel rather hopeless about it.

The first psychotherapy treatment that was shown to be effective was exposure therapy, which essentially encourages people in a graded way to go into their feared situations and stay in them as long as they can and build up their confidence that way. Often, the therapist will accompany the person to a feared situation to provide support and guidance. Group cognitive behaviour therapy has also been shown to be effective. This is a talking therapy that helps people to understand the link between negative thoughts and mood and how altering their behaviour can enable them to manage anxiety and feel in control.

There are, of course, drugs that can help people with anxiety. Medication will not cure an anxiety disorder, but it can keep it under control while the person receives psychotherapy. The principal medications used for anxiety disorders are antidepressants, anti-anxiety drugs, and beta-blockers to control some of the physical symptoms. With proper treatment, many people with anxiety disorders can lead normal, fulfilling lives.

There is plenty of evidence that exercise can help with anxiety problems. When stress affects the brain, with its many nerve connections, the rest of the body feels the impact as well. Exercise and other physical activity produce endorphins, which are chemicals in the brain that act as natural painkillers. In addition to this, getting physically tired can help people fall asleep faster and have deeper and more relaxing sleep. As many people suffering from anxiety often have problems with insomnia, just the ability to get a good night's rest can change people's whole perspectives.

Anxiety is a normal, but highly subjective, human emotion. While normal anxiety serves a beneficial and adaptive purpose, anxiety can also become the cause of tremendous suffering for millions of people. It is important that people recognise excessive anxiety in themselves as soon as possible, as treatment can be very successful and living untreated can be a misery.

Glossary

Amygdala - a section of the brain that is responsible for detecting fear.

Questions 1 – 3

*Complete each sentence with the correct ending (**A - E**) below. Write the correct letter (**A - E**) in answer boxes **1 - 3** on your answer sheet.*

1   Experiencing small doses of anxiety can

2   Imagining or exaggerating problems can

3   Nearly one in five people can

A   be very beneficial.

B   never have to deal with anxiety

C   lead to unhelpful levels of anxiety.

D   experience anxiety at some point.

E   increase the possibility of physical disease.

Questions 4 – 6

Answer the questions below.

Write **NO MORE THAN THREE WORDS AND/OR A NUMBER** from the text for each answer.

Write your answers in boxes **4 - 6** on your answer sheet.

4   Which area of the brain have scientists identified as being significant in anxiety problems?

5   What proportion of people look for treatment for their anxiety?

6   What part of themselves do most people blame for their anxiety?

Questions 7 – 13

Complete the table below.

Write **NO MORE THAN TWO WORDS** from the text for each answer.

Write your answers in boxes **7 - 13** on your answer sheet.

Treatment for Anxiety	
Exposure Therapy	Patients face their fears in a (**7**) _____ fashion, often with their (**8**) _____.
Group Cognitive Behaviour Therapy	A talking therapy. It explores the links between (**9**) _____and feelings. It explores how changing people's (**10**) _____ can help them regain control.
Drugs	These cannot cure people, but they can help in conjunction with (**11**) _____.
Exercise	By creating (**12**) _____, the body can help dull the pain of anxiety. It can allow a good sleep for people who suffer from the (**13**) _____ caused by their anxiety.

READING PASSAGE 2

*You should spend about 20 minutes on **Questions 14 - 26**, which are based on Reading Passage 2 below.*

The Grand Banks

Paragraph A
The Grand Banks is a large area of submerged highlands southeast of Newfoundland and east of the Laurentian Channel on the North American continental shelf. Covering 93,200 square kilometres, the Grand Banks are relatively shallow, ranging from 25 to 100 meters in depth. It is in this area that the cold Labrador Current mixes with the warm waters of the Gulf Stream. The mixing of these waters and the shape of the ocean bottom lifts nutrients to the surface and these conditions created one of the richest fishing grounds in the world. Extensive marine life flourishes in the Grand Banks, whose range extends beyond the Canadian 200-mile exclusive economic zone (EEZ) and into international waters. This has made it an important part of both the Canadian and the high seas fisheries, with fishermen risking their lives in the extremely inhospitable environment consisting of rogue waves, fog, icebergs, sea ice, hurricanes, winter storms and earthquakes.

Paragraph B
While the area's 'official' discovery is credited to John Cabot in 1497, English and Portuguese vessels are known to have first sought out these waters prior to that, based upon reports they received from earlier Viking voyages to Newfoundland. Several navigators, including Basque fishermen, are known to have fished these waters in the fifteenth century. Some texts from that era refer to a land called *Bacalao*, 'the land of the codfish', which is possibly Newfoundland. However, it was not until John Cabot noted the waters' abundance of sea life that the existence of these fishing grounds became widely known in Europe. Soon, fishermen and merchants from France, Spain, Portugal and England developed seasonal inshore fisheries producing for European markets. Known as 'dry' fishery, cod were split, salted, and dried on shore over the summer before crews returned to Europe. The French pioneered 'wet' or 'green' fishery on the Grand Banks proper around 1550, heavily salting the cod on board and immediately returning home.

Paragraph C
The Grand Banks were possibly the world's most important international fishing area in the nineteenth and twentieth centuries. Technological advances in fishing, such as sonar and large factory ships, including the massive factory freezer trawlers introduced in the 1950's, led to overfishing and a serious decline in the fish stocks. Based upon the many foreign policy agreements Newfoundland had entered into prior to its admittance into the Canadian Confederation, foreign fleets, some from as far away as Russia, came to the Grand Banks in force, catching unprecedented quantities of fish.

Paragraph D

Between 1973 and 1982, the United Nations and its member states negotiated the Third Convention of the Law of the Sea, one component of which was the concept of nations being allowed to declare an EEZ. Many nations worldwide-declared 200-nautical mile EEZ's, including Canada and the United States. On the whole, the EEZ was very well received by fishermen in eastern Canada, because it meant they could fish unhindered out to the limit without fear of competing with the foreign fleets. During the late 1970's and early 1980s, Canada's domestic offshore fleet grew as fishermen and fish processing companies rushed to take advantage. It was during this time that it was noticed that the foreign fleets now pushed out to areas of the Grand Banks off Newfoundland outside the Canadian EEZ. By the late 1980's, dwindling catches of Atlantic cod were being reported throughout Newfoundland and eastern Canada, and the federal government and citizens of coastal regions in the area began to face the reality that the domestic and foreign overfishing had taken its toll. The Canadian government was finally forced to take drastic action in 1992, when a total moratorium was declared indefinitely for the northern cod.

Paragraph E

Over the last ten years, it has been noted that cod appear to be returning to the Grand Banks in small numbers. The reasons for this fragile recovery are still unknown. Perhaps, the damage done by trawlers is not permanent and the marine fauna and ecosystems can rebuild themselves if given a prolonged period of time without any commercial activity. Either way, the early stage recovery of the Grand Banks is encouraging news, but caution is needed, as, after nearly twenty years of severe limitations, cod stocks are still only at approximately ten per cent of 1960's levels. It is hoped that in another ten to twenty years, stocks may be close to a full recovery, although this would require political pressure to maintain strict limitations on commercial fishing. If cod do come back to the Grand Banks in meaningful numbers, it is to be hoped that the Canadians will not make the same mistakes again.

Paragraph F

Further riches have now been found in the Grand Banks. Petroleum reserves have been discovered and a number of oil fields are under development in the region. The vast Hibernia oil field was discovered in 1979, and, following several years of aborted start-up attempts, the Hibernia megaproject began construction of the production platform and gravity base structures in the early 1990's. Production commenced on November 17, 1997, with initial production rates in excess of 50,000 barrels of crude oil per day from a single well. Hibernia has proven to be the most prolific oil well in Canada. However, earthquake and iceberg activity in the Grand Banks pose a potential ecological disaster that could devastate the fishing grounds that are only now starting to recover.

Questions 14 – 20

*The text on the previous pages has 6 paragraphs **A - F**.*

Which paragraph contains the following information?

*Write your answers in boxes **14 – 20** on your answer sheet.*

14   Many countries could legally fish Newfoundland waters because of treaties Newfoundland had made before becoming part of Canada.

15   The establishment of the EEZ did not stop over-fishing in the Grand Banks.

16   Natural disasters could cause oil to destroy what is left of the Grand Banks ecosystem.

17   The original amount of fish in the Grand Banks was due to different temperature waters mixing.

18   East Canadian fishermen were generally happy with the establishment of the Canadian EEZ.

19   Grand Banks' cod stocks are still 90 per cent lower than what they were in the 1960's.

20   The French were the first to prepare the cod on board their ships before going back to France.

Questions 21 – 23

*Choose the correct letter **A, B, C or D**.*

*Write the correct letter in boxes **21 - 23** on your answer sheet.*

21   The first English fishermen to come to the Grand Banks to fish

    A   were told about the fishery by Basque fishermen.
    B   were sent word about the fishery from the first American colonists.
    C   acted on information from previous Viking expeditions.
    D   discovered the fishery themselves while exploring.

22   John Cabot's reports of the Grand Banks

    A   led to the establishment of the Canadian EEZ.
    B   meant the fishery was well known in Europe.
    C   led to fighting between rival fishing fleets.
    D   were not immediately publicised, so that English fishermen could benefit.

23   The establishment of the Canadian EEZ

    A   did not stop foreign fishermen from fishing the Grand Banks.
    B   was not ratified by the United Nations.
    C   temporarily stopped the over-fishing of cod in the Grand Banks.
    D   meant Canadian fishermen were excluded from fishing the Grand Banks.

Questions 24 – 26

Do the following statements agree with the information given in the text?

*In boxes **24 – 26** on your answer sheet write:*

    TRUE   *if the statement agrees with the information*
    FALSE   *if the statement contradicts the information*
    NOT GIVEN   *if there is no information on this*

24   Even now, cod stocks have shown no signs of recovery in the Grand Banks.

25   Initial efforts to extract oil from the Grand Banks' Hibernia oil field were unsuccessful.

26   Oil exploration companies have to follow strict safety controls imposed by the Canadian government.

READING PASSAGE 3

*You should spend about 20 minutes on **Questions 27 - 40**, which are based on Reading Passage 3 below.*

An Aging Population

People are living longer and, in some parts of the world, healthier lives. This represents one of the crowning achievements of the last century, but also a significant challenge. Longer lives must be planned for. Societal aging may affect economic growth and lead to many other issues, including the sustainability of families, the ability of states and communities to provide resources for older citizens, and international relations. *The Global Burden of Disease*, a study conducted by the World Health Organization, predicts a very large increase in age-related chronic disease in all regions of the world. Dealing with this will be a significant challenge for all countries' health services.

Population aging is driven by declines in fertility and improvements in health and longevity. In more developed countries, falling fertility beginning in the early 1900's has resulted in current levels being below the population replacement rate of two live births per woman. Perhaps the most surprising demographic development of the past 20 years has been the pace of fertility decline in many less developed countries. In 2006, for example, the total fertility rate was at or below the replacement rate in 44 less developed countries.

One central issue for policymakers in regard to pension funds is the relationship between the official retirement age and actual retirement age. Over several decades in the latter part of the 20th century, many of the more developed nations lowered the official age at which people become fully entitled to public pension benefits. This was propelled by general economic conditions, changes in welfare philosophy, and private pension trends. Despite the recent trend toward increased workforce participation at older ages, a significant gap between official and actual ages of retirement persists. This trend is emerging in rapidly aging developing countries as well. Many countries already have taken steps towards much-needed reform of their old-age social insurance programs. One common reform has been to raise the age at which workers are eligible for full public pension benefits. Another strategy for bolstering economic security for older people has been to increase the contributions by workers. Other measures to enhance income for older people include new financial instruments for private savings, tax incentives for individual retirement savings, and supplemental occupational pension plans.

As life expectancy increases in most nations, so do the odds of different generations within a family coexisting. In more developed countries, this has manifested itself as the 'beanpole family,' a vertical extension of family structure characterised by an increase in the number of living generations within a lineage and a decrease in the number of people within each generation. As mortality rates continue to improve, more people in their 50's and 60's will have surviving parents, aunts, and uncles. Consequently, more children will know their grandparents and even their great-grandparents, especially their great-grandmothers. There is no historical precedent for a majority of middle-aged and older adults having living parents.

As the World Health Organisation study, *The Global Burden of Disease*, predicts that in a few decades the loss of health and life worldwide will be greater from non-communicable or chronic diseases than from infectious diseases, childhood diseases, and accidents. The study estimates that today, non-communicable diseases account for 85 per cent of the burden of disease in high-income countries and a surprising 44 per cent of the burden of disease in low- and middle-income countries. Non-communicable diseases already account for as much of the burden of disease in low- and middle-income countries as all communicable diseases, maternal and perinatal conditions, and nutritional conditions. By 2030, according to projections, the share of the burden attributed to non-communicable diseases in low- and middle-income countries will reach 54 per cent, while the share attributed to communicable diseases will fall to 32 per cent. If we restrict attention to older ages, non-communicable diseases already account for more than 87 per cent of the burden for the over-60 population in low-, middle-, and high-income countries. The critical issue for low- and middle-income countries is how to mobilise and allocate resources to address non-communicable diseases, as they continue to struggle with the continued high prevalence of communicable diseases. Of course, a significant jump in disability numbers has accompanied the increase in longevity.

Because countries age at different paces, it is possible for the elements of production - labour and capital - to flow across national boundaries and mitigate the impact of population aging. Studies predict that, in the near term, surplus capital will flow from Europe and North America to emerging markets in Asia and Latin America, where the population is younger and cheaper and supplies of capital relatively low. In another 20 years, when the baby boom generation in the West has mostly retired, capital will most likely flow in the opposite direction. However, these studies rest on the uncertain assumption that capital will flow easily across national boundaries.

Despite the weight of scientific evidence, the significance of population aging and its global implications have yet to be wholly appreciated. There is a need to raise awareness about not only global aging issues, but also the importance of rigorous cross-national scientific research and policy dialogue that will help us address the challenges and opportunities of an aging world. Preparing financially for longer lives and finding ways to reduce aging-related disability should become national and global priorities. Experience shows that for nations, as for individuals, it is critical to address problems sooner rather than later. Waiting significantly increases the costs and difficulties of addressing these challenges.

Questions 27 – 33

Complete the notes below.

Write **NO MORE THAN THREE WORDS** *for each answer.*

Write your answers in boxes **27 - 33** *on your answer sheet.*

An Aging Population

* The longer lives of people of today must be prepared for.

* The longer lives will affect economics, family life, old age care and health services.

* The aging population has been caused by a drop in fertility, improvements in health and

(**27**) _____; the former is surprisingly seen in many (**28**) _____.

* One key area to consider is the age for retirement benefits to be paid – this has changed a

lot recently in (**29**) _____, due to various conditions and trends.

* A lot of (**30**) _____ is required in many countries and some have already done this –

usually by raising the official pension age or raising the (**31**) _____ of people still

working.

* Other new financial instruments have also been launched.

* Longer life expectancy will also lead to different family (**32**) _____ living with each

other more.

* There has been no previous (**33**) _____ of such a change in family demographics.

Questions 34 – 39

Do the following statements agree with the views of the writer of the text?

In boxes 34 - 39 on your answer sheet write:

YES	*if the statement agrees with the writer's views*
NO	*if the statement doesn't agree with the writer's views*
NOT GIVEN	*if it is impossible to say what the writer thinks about this*

34   It is no shock that low- and middle-income countries have experienced a significant rise in non-communicable diseases.

35   While the numbers of people with chronic diseases have increased around the world, the numbers of people with disability problems have reduced.

36   It is theorised that money invested short-term in Asia will later be reinvested back in the West.

37   It is predicted that problems in the international flow of capital will lead to armed conflict between some countries.

38   All the effects of population aging around the world have still not been fully realised.

39   It would be better to wait a while to see how the situation develops, as fast decisions could create problems in the future.

Question 40

*Choose the correct letter, **A, B, C or D**.*

*Write the correct letter in box **40** on your answer sheet.*

40   What is the writer's purpose in Reading Passage 3?

A   To provide suggestions on how developed countries can deal with their aging populations.

B   To provide an overview of the causes and effects of the world's aging population.

C   To provide potential suggestions on how to prevent the world's aging population from increasing.

D   To provide a historical analysis of the causes of today's aging population.

WRITING

WRITING TASK 1

You should spend about 20 minutes on this task.

The bar chart below shows Scotland's exports to the rest of the UK and the rest of the world for the year 2014.

Summarise the information by selecting and reporting the main features, and make comparisons where relevant.

You should write at least 150 words.

Scotland's Exports to the Rest of the UK and the Rest of the World - 2014

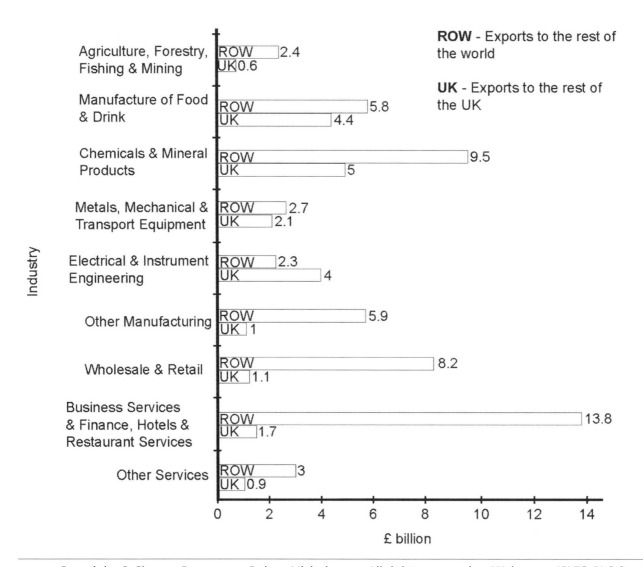

WRITING TASK 2

You should spend about 40 minutes on this task.

Write about the following topic:

> **Many parents today organise extra classes for their children after school and at the weekends.**
>
> **Do you feel that this is a worthwhile thing to do or do you feel children have enough education at school?**

Give reasons for your answer and include any relevant examples from your knowledge or experience.

You should write at least 250 words.

SPEAKING

SECTION 1

- Can you describe your old school to me?
- How did you get to school every day?
- Did you enjoy your experience at school? (Why/Why not?)

Topic 1   The Seasons

- Which is your favourite season?
- What sports are popular in different seasons in your country?
- In which season do you think it's best to get married?
- What problems are caused by extreme seasonal weather?

Topic 2   Languages

- Is the language in your country difficult to learn?
- What languages are learned at schools in your country?
- What are the advantages of speaking more than one language?
- When you visit a foreign country, do you try and learn some of the language? (Why/Why not?)

SECTION 2

Describe a sport or game that you like to watch or play.
You should say:
        why you like to watch or play this sport or game
        where you watch or play this sport or game
        how much it costs to watch or play this sport or game
and briefly explain how the game is played.

SECTION 3

Topic 1   Exercise and Health

- Why is doing exercise good for you?
- How can we get young people to exercise more?
- How can sport improve people's mental health?
- How can sport be bad for your health?

Topic 2   Sport and Money

- How have trends in sport changed over the last 50 years?
- Do you think that top sportsmen and women are sometimes overpaid? (Why/Why not?)
- How do you feel about betting and sport?
- How important is the relationship between sport and advertising?

PRACTICE TEST 12

LISTENING

 Download audio recordings for the test here:
http://www.ielts-blog.com/ielts-practice-tests-downloads/

SECTION 1   *Questions 1 – 10*

Questions 1 – 5

*Circle the correct letters **A - C**.*

> **Example**
>
> Graham and Sophie's holiday will begin in
> **(A)**   Oban.
> **B**   Skye.
> **C**   Lewis.

1   Graham and Sophie's first night in Oban is on the

    A   7th July.
    B   8th July.
    C   13th July.

2   Graham and Sophie plan to travel to Oban by

    A   car.
    B   bus.
    C   train.

3   Sophie said that she'd check places to stay in, but

    A   she only ordered some magazines.
    B   she didn't do anything.
    C   she only checked a few things on the internet.

4   In Oban, Graham and Sophie will stay

    A   in a hostel.
    B   in a guest house.
    C   in a hotel.

5   Graham and Sophie's booking for accommodation will include

    A   breakfast but not dinner.
    B   breakfast and dinner.
    C   neither breakfast nor dinner.

Questions 6 – 10

Complete Sophie's table notes below on her hiking holiday.

Write **NO MORE THAN ONE WORD OR A NUMBER** from the listening for each answer.

	Hike 1	Hike 2
Where	Oban to Dunbeg	Island of Kerrera
Difficulty	Easy (no (**6**) _____)	Easy
Distance	Along coast for 3½ hours	About (**8**) _____ miles in length
Sights	The sea, island of Kerrera, cathedral and a spectacular ruined castle	Land and some sea views; castle
Notes	Lunch in Dunbeg and then take a (**7**) _____ home (around 15 minutes)	Go slowly - look around the castle and have a (**9**) _____
We can buy a (**10**) _____ on the ferry.		

SECTION 2   *Questions 11 - 20*

Questions 11 and 12

*Choose **TWO** letters, **A - F**.*

Where did the money come from to buy the town's new museum's building?

A   from the local Weyport town council

B   from money collected from the general public

C   from the previous town museum

D   from the previous museum director

E   from a local business

F   from the central arts council

Questions 13 – 15

*Choose **THREE** letters, **A - G**.*

What has the town's new museum's building been used for since it was built?

A   An office building

B   The fire service

C   An insurance company

D   Keeping council property

E   An army centre

F   The council education department

G   The council housing department

Questions 16 – 20

*Below is a plan of the Weyport Museum ground floor with **9** locations marked **A - I**.*
*Questions **16 - 20** name **5** things that can be seen or visited in the museum.*
*Write the correct letter (**A - I**) that matches the things with their locations.*

16   The bathrooms   _____

17   Paintings   _____

18   Silverware   _____

19   Film   _____

20   Toys   _____

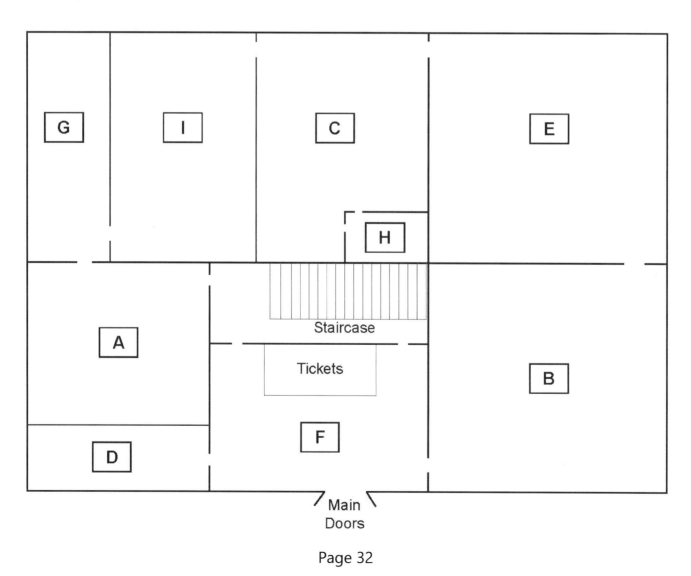

SECTION 3   *Questions 21 – 30*

Questions 21 – 25

Complete the flow chart that summarises the students' planning of their field trip.

*Choose **FIVE** answers from the list below (**A** - **H**) and write the correct letter next to questions **21** - **25**.*

A	location	**E**	accommodation
B	equipment	**F**	dates
C	computer	**G**	provisions
D	transport	**H**	duration

Cliff Formation Survey Field Trip

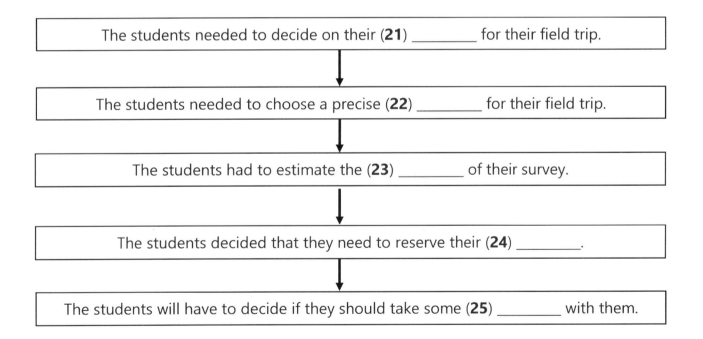

The students needed to decide on their (**21**) _____ for their field trip.

↓

The students needed to choose a precise (**22**) _____ for their field trip.

↓

The students had to estimate the (**23**) _____ of their survey.

↓

The students decided that they need to reserve their (**24**) _____.

↓

The students will have to decide if they should take some (**25**) _____ with them.

Questions 26 – 28

Complete the diagram below on the students' target area of coastal cliff erosion.

Write **NO MORE THAN TWO WORDS** from the listening for each answer.

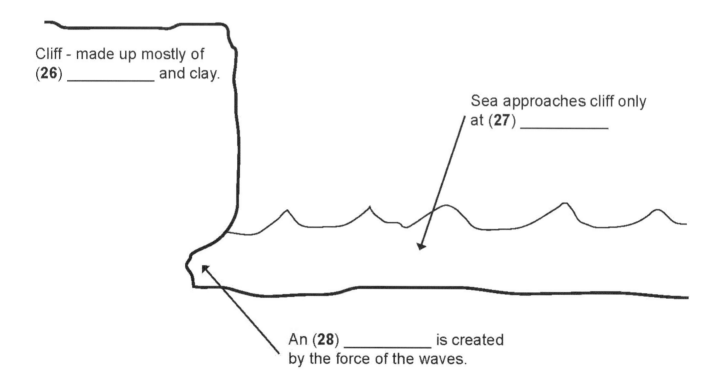

Cliff - made up mostly of
(**26**) _____ and clay.

Sea approaches cliff only
at (**27**) _____

An (**28**) _____ is created
by the force of the waves.

Questions 29 and 30

Answer the questions below.

Use **NO MORE THAN THREE WORDS** from the listening for each answer.

29   Which organisation monitors the coastal cliff erosion where the students will be going?

30   What does Alan say the students should bring in case they run into any danger?

SECTION 4   *Questions 31 – 40*

Questions 31 – 40

Complete the summary below on the lecture on the Wechsler-Belleview Intelligence Scale.

*Write **NO MORE THAN TWO WORDS** from the listening for each answer.*

The Wechsler-Belleview Intelligence Scale (The WBIS)

Wechsler believed intelligence was made up of different skills considered within the context of the (**31**) _____. His intelligence scale broke away from existing intelligence tests and set up a numerical scale with the (**32**) _____ set at 100.

Wechsler decided to create a test to measure these different skills that made up intelligence. The 2 main areas tested were (**33**) _____ and performance and these were then broken down to 14 sub-tests, 7 for each. These 14 topics remain the basis for today's WBIS, which is today's most commonly used (**34**) _____.

The WBIS is aimed at adults; for younger children other related scales are used, neither of which need (**35**) _____ in a child.

The WBIS is not suitable for assessing (**36**) _____ of intelligence or of the age range. For any of these situations, care should be taken with (**37**) _____ of the results.

The WBIS can also be used for neuropsychological assessment. Differences in answers can indicate types of (**38**) _____. In addition, the WBIS is used to diagnose learning disabilities and ADHD. Although experts say the WBIS is best used only for intelligence, it is used to compare cognitive development and performance in social skills or at (**39**) _____.

The WBIS is highly regarded as an intelligence test and is often used as a point of comparison for other tests when assessing their (**40**) _____ and validity.

READING

READING PASSAGE 1

*You should spend about 20 minutes on **Questions 1 - 13**, which are based on Reading Passage 1 below.*

The Igloo

The igloo is the traditional shelter of Inuit living in the far northern regions. They are built of blocks of snow in a circular shape, in which the walls curve inward towards the top to form a snow vault with a self-supporting arched ceiling. An outstanding example of human ingenuity and adaptability to the environment, the igloo retains heat and protects against the cold, since snow and ice act as excellent insulation. The design includes a tunnel entrance that forms a cold trap to preserve heat inside. The sleeping and sitting areas are raised above this and so maintain a higher temperature.

A similar construction is the 'quinzhee', which is a shelter made by hollowing out a pile of settled snow, and is only for temporary use. In contemporary times, this type of snow shelter has become popular among those who enjoy winter camping, as well as in survival situations. Some contemporary Inuit though continue to use igloos, especially as temporary shelters while hunting. However, the warming climate of the early twenty-first century has reduced the availability of appropriate snow for igloo construction. Although the traditional art of igloo construction by Inuit natives may have declined, the igloo and variations upon it, such as ice hotels, have gained in popularity among those who enjoy the winter experience.

An igloo in the Inuit language simply means house and the Inuit do not restrict the use of this term exclusively to snow houses, but include traditional tents, sod houses, homes constructed of driftwood, and modern buildings. Although the origin of the igloo may have been lost in antiquity, it is known that Inuit have constructed snow igloos for hundreds of years. Living in an area where snow and ice predominate, particularly in the long dark winter above the Arctic Circle, the igloo is the perfect shelter. Snow is used because the air pockets trapped in it make it an excellent insulator. Outside, temperatures may be as low as minus 45 degrees Celsius, but inside an igloo, the temperature may range from minus 7 degrees Celsius to 16 degrees Celsius when warmed by body heat alone. A highly functional shelter, the igloo is also aesthetically pleasing, with its shape being both strong and beautiful.

In order to build an igloo, there is a fairly standard procedure. The first thing to do is to find a good spot. It is vital to choose a safe location away from avalanche prone slopes. Next, mark a circle in the snow. For two people, a circle of around two metres diameter is needed, and for four people, around four metres. The igloo body is the next step. Shovel a pile of snow into a large, reasonably steep mound and try and keep the sloping sides at an angle of around 35 degrees or higher, which is best for stability. Wide, short snow shelters are more prone to collapse. If possible, mix snow of different temperatures to help it to harden. The entrance is done by digging a trench downwards into the snow towards the mound. This should be on the downhill side and out of the wind. The snow that is being removed from the trench should be placed on top of the mound. In these conditions, make the trench as deep as a standing man. Then, leave everything for about 90 minutes if possible. Next, finish the tunnel entrance. Make the tunnel slightly wider than a body's width and dig at a slightly upward angle. Ideally, the floor of the snow shelter should be at least 30 centimetres above the entrance, which will help prevent warm air from escaping the shelter. After the initial entrance is made, it is easier to hollow the inside from the top down. The walls should be thirty to sixty centimetres thick, and if the inside walls are smoothed, this will help prevent dripping. Leave an elevated platform for sleeping on. As heat rises, the occupants will be in the warmest part of the igloo for sleeping. A very important point is to make an air vent in the wall of the shelter, which will prevent the occupants from suffocating in the night. Finally, block the entrance with a block of snow or a rucksack.

Igloo hotels are a new variation on the traditional igloo. In several winter destinations, villages of igloos are built for tourists, where the guests use sleeping bags that sit on top of reindeer hides in overnight stays. Ice hotels are found in many places in Norway, Finland, and Sweden, and are constructed each winter and melt in the spring. The Ice Hotel in the village of Jukkasjärvi, located next to the town of Kiruna in Sweden, is a famous attraction. Originally, the creators started out building a simple igloo, which later turned into the elaborate and now famous 'hotel'. It is made from the waters of the adjacent river Torne, the pure waters of which produce beautiful clear ice used to create interior decorations, which are made entirely of snow and ice.

The igloo is a subject that has fascinated people from all over the world. Although the traditional art of igloo construction by Inuit natives may have declined, the igloo and variations on it have gained in popularity among those who enjoy the novelty and winter experience.

Glossary

Inuit - native people of the northern regions of Canada, North America and Greenland.

Questions 1 – 3

Do the following statements agree with the information given in the text?

In boxes **1 – 3** on your answer sheet write:

TRUE	if the statement agrees with the information
FALSE	if the statement contradicts the information
NOT GIVEN	if there is no information on this

1   The quinzhee is constructed for living in long-term.

2   The Canadian government has allocated grants to keep the art of building igloos alive.

3   Although relatively warm, the temperature inside an igloo in winter Arctic conditions will never rise above freezing.

Questions 4 – 10

Complete the flow chart below. Write **NO MORE THAN TWO WORDS** from the text for each answer. Write your answers in boxes **4 – 10** on your answer sheet.

Building An Igloo

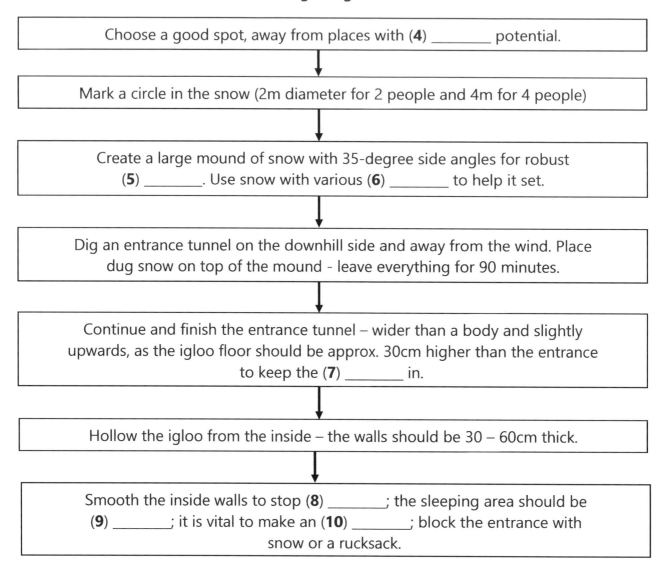

Choose a good spot, away from places with (**4**) _____ potential.

↓

Mark a circle in the snow (2m diameter for 2 people and 4m for 4 people)

↓

Create a large mound of snow with 35-degree side angles for robust (**5**) _____. Use snow with various (**6**) _____ to help it set.

↓

Dig an entrance tunnel on the downhill side and away from the wind. Place dug snow on top of the mound - leave everything for 90 minutes.

↓

Continue and finish the entrance tunnel – wider than a body and slightly upwards, as the igloo floor should be approx. 30cm higher than the entrance to keep the (**7**) _____ in.

↓

Hollow the igloo from the inside – the walls should be 30 – 60cm thick.

↓

Smooth the inside walls to stop (**8**) _____; the sleeping area should be (**9**) _____; it is vital to make an (**10**) _____; block the entrance with snow or a rucksack.

Questions 11 – 13

Complete the summary below. Write **NO MORE THAN TWO WORDS** from the text for each answer. Write your answers in boxes **11 - 13** on your answer sheet.

The Jukkasjärvi Ice Hotel

Igloo hotels are popular novelties, where guests can sleep in sleeping bags on (**11**) _____ . These hotels (in northern countries) are built every year and (**12**) _____ when it warms. The famous Jukkasjärvi Ice Hotel is completely made from nearby river water - even the (**13**) _____ .

READING PASSAGE 2

*You should spend about 20 minutes on **Questions 14 - 26**, which are based on Reading Passage 2 below.*

Computer Viruses

Computers can do anything: from running spread sheets, word processors and power stations to music synthesisers and missile control systems. And because computers can do anything, they can in particular run viruses and any other nasty software.

Viruses are unique in their abilities, as they can stop many computers at once. This would be much more serious for a small company than normal faults that affect only one PC at a time. Thus, viruses rank with hazards like power cuts and fire in their effect and speed of action. Worse than fire though, people may find that they cannot take their work elsewhere, for if they did, they might simply take the virus infection with them and bring more systems down. Secondly, viruses can distribute disinformation and bring shame to individuals or organisations: viruses may send malicious email apparently on behalf of the person whose computer has been infected.

A computer virus is a piece of program code that attaches copies of itself to other programs, incorporating itself into them, so that the modified programs, while still possibly performing their intended function, surreptitiously do other things. Programs so corrupted seek others to which to attach the virus, and so the infection circulates. Successful viruses lie low until they have thoroughly infiltrated the system, and only reveal their presence when they cause damage. The effect of a virus is rarely linked back to its originator, so viruses make attractive weapons for vandals. Computer viruses generally work by altering files that contain otherwise harmless programs. This is infection. When an infected program is invoked, it seeks other programs stored in files to which it has write permission, and infects them by modifying the files to include a copy of itself and inserting an instruction to branch to that code at the old program's starting point. Then the virus starts up the original program, so that the user is unaware of its intervention. Viruses are classified as being one of two types: 'research' or 'in the wild'. A research virus is one that has been written for research or study purposes and has received almost no distribution to the public. On the other hand, viruses that have been seen with any regularity are termed 'in the wild'.

Before the spread of the Internet, most computer viruses were spread by removable media, predominantly floppy disks. Some viruses spread by infecting programs stored on these disks, while others installed themselves into the disk boot sector. Until floppy disks were replaced by other removable media, this was the most successful infection strategy and boot sector viruses were the most common in the wild for many years.

The term 'computer virus' is a popular catchall for all kinds of malicious software. A logic bomb is a destructive program activated by a certain combination of circumstances, or on a certain date, to delete information. A Trojan horse is any bug inserted into a computer program that takes advantage of the trusted status of its host by surreptitiously performing unintended functions. A worm is a distributed program that invades computers on a network. It consists of several processes or segments that keep in touch through the network; when one is lost, the others conspire to replace it on another server.

Viruses today have no distinct identity, but typically undergo mutation each time they copy themselves to other files. This, combined with various cryptographic techniques, makes modern viruses difficult to detect. False alarms have become an increasing problem, particularly with users sending chain email warning about supposed virus problems; ironically, the panics may cause more problems than the viruses they warn about. Email though has become the most popular way to disperse viruses today, because powerful commercial email packages are themselves programmable and users often configure email systems to helpfully run programs automatically.

Viruses are not difficult to develop. The majority of viruses are simple variants of others and many virus construction kits are readily available on the Internet. Viruses have been created since the 1960's, although the term 'computer virus' was only formally defined by Fred Cohen in 1983. One of the first virus attacks occurred in late 1987 when, over a two-month period, a virus quietly insinuated itself into programs at a Middle East university. It was noticed because it caused programs to grow longer. Once discovered, it was analysed and an antidote devised. It was designed to slow processors down on certain Fridays, and to erase all files on Friday, 13 May.

It is common that certain viruses have been given names. Once discovered and named, programmers can create 'antidotes' that delete the viruses from the system. The obvious, but generally impractical defence against viruses is never to use anyone else's software and never to connect with anyone else's computer. A more practical approach to protect computers is to regularly or continuously run programs that recognise viruses and try to eliminate virus infections before they do too much damage. Because new viruses are being devised every day, it is important and sensible to keep detection programs up to date, by, for example, a regular subscription from a reputable firm, and to minimise risky procedures, such as sharing information as infrequently as possible.

All protection approaches are trade-offs. Eternal vigilance on the part of users is important, and, above all, education of users to the possible results of their actions.

Questions 14 – 18

Complete the summary using the words in the box below.

*Write your answers in boxes **14 - 18** on your answer sheet.*

COMPUTER VIRUSES

Computers today can perform all tasks, including running computer viruses. Viruses are worse than other computer problems, due to their ability to (**14**) _____ to other systems. Viruses can also circulate misrepresentations and the (**15**) _____ of people and groups can be harmed.

Computer viruses are pieces of program code that become part of programs and then spread to other programs and computers. They usually (**16**) _____ themselves within systems before creating harm and their (**17**) _____ are difficult to trace. Viruses also distribute themselves around files and computers without being noticed. Viruses can be 'research' or 'in the wild', the former usually creating no (**18**) _____.

---

recipes	kill	spread	origins	die
cures	reputations	hide	jobs	risks

Questions 19 – 23

Answer the questions below.

*Write **NO MORE THAN THREE WORDS** from the text for each answer.*

*Write your answers in boxes **19 - 23** on your answer sheet.*

19   What type of removable media was first responsible for the distribution of computer viruses?

20   What type of computer virus can be set to delete information at a particular time?

21   What type of computer virus attacks networked computers?

22   What combines with various cryptographic techniques to make a modern computer virus difficult to discover?

23   What is the most common way to distribute a computer virus nowadays?

Questions 24 – 26

Complete the sentences below.

*Write **NO MORE THAN THREE WORDS** from the text for each answer.*

*Write your answers in boxes **24 - 26** on your answer sheet.*

24   Most viruses are just simple _____ of pre-existing viruses.

25   _____ to a trustworthy company that deals in virus protection is a practical precaution against computer viruses.

26   The key action to avoid computer viruses is the _____, so that they appreciate the potential consequences of what they do.

READING PASSAGE 3

*You should spend about 20 minutes on **Questions 27 - 40**, which are based on Reading Passage 3 below.*

Homeschooling

Paragraph A

Homeschooling is a method of education where children do not attend a traditional school. Instead, usually parents take over the responsibility for the education of their children, either doing it all themselves or by using a company that specialises in providing homeschooling curricula and materials. Homeschooled children can excel in standardised testing and universities and colleges have no qualms about accepting them. Supporters also claim that because they have been trained early on to be independent learners, homeschooled individuals grow up to become reliable, resourceful individuals.

Paragraph B

Homeschooling offers various benefits. Almost all homeschooling families say that homeschooling has played an essential role in bringing their family closer, as the time that parents spend teaching their children, and the time the children spend learning together, can foster a loving relationship in the family. Homeschooled children do not have to worry about bullying, peer pressure and spiteful competition, so their self-esteem does not have to suffer needlessly, and many parents with children who have been the target of bullying have resorted to homeschooling to protect their children from the harmful effects of harassment. Another key advantage of homeschooling is that parents and children no longer have to work their lives around homework and school hours. They usually accomplish in a few hours each day what typically takes a week or more to complete in a classroom setting. Because they spend more time in hands-on learning, homeschooled children can do away with homework, which is what usually keeps public schooled children up late at night. Additionally, families can schedule off-season vacations, go on field trips or visit museums, zoos and parks during the week as part of their learning experience. A more controversial benefit of homeschooling is that parents have frequently much more say in what is taught to their children, so that they can avoid subjects which they disapprove of.

Paragraph C

Homeschooling is, however, sharply criticised in some quarters. A common criticism is that homeschooled children may not have as many opportunities to interact with other children in comparison to children who attend regular schools. Forming bonds and socialising with children his or her own age is important for a child's developmental health and development of social skills. If homeschooled, children may be deprived of the chance to form friendships and may suffer socially. The lack of socialisation may affect them in later stages of life.

Paragraph D

Parents choosing to homeschool their children may also be faced with the common problem of time. Parents need to set aside time to make it work. The task of homeschooling a child is certainly not easy, whether for working parents, single parents or stay-at-home parents. They have to take time to organise and prepare lessons, teach, give tests, and plan field trips. Also, in comparison to public schools where education is free, homeschooling can also be costly, as purchasing the newest curriculum and teaching tools can be very expensive. Parents may choose to use a pre-prepared paid homeschooling program, but, in spite of the possible added benefits of such programs, they may increase the cost of the child's education. There are also other costs to keep in mind, like project materials, stationery, books, computer software, and field trips.

Paragraph E
There is also the issue of the different relationships between parents and their children and teachers and their students. Public and private schools provide for many children a safe haven, in which they are both regarded and respected independently and individually. Family love is intense, and children need it to survive and thrive. It is also deeply contingent on the existence and nature of the family ties. The unconditional love children receive at home is actually anything but unconditional: it is conditioned on the fact that they are their parents' children. School, either public or private, ideally provides a welcome respite. Children are regarded and respected at school not because they are their parents' children, but because they are students. They are valued for traits and for status that are independent of their status as the parents' genetic or adoptive offspring. The ideal teacher cares about a child as an individual, a learner and an actively curious person. The teacher does not care about the child because the child is his or hers, and the child is regarded with respect equal to all the children in the class. In these ways, the school classroom, ideally, and the relations within it, is a model of some core aspects of citizenship.

Paragraph F
A final criticism of homeschooling is that there is a public health risk. Children who attend public schools are required to have immunisations in order to begin classes. It is hard in many countries to ensure that mandatory immunisation is verified. Thus, deregulated homeschooling means that homeschooled children are basically exempted from immunisation requirements. The children are more susceptible to the diseases against which immunisation gives some protection, and others around them, particularly the elderly, are also consequently in danger.

Paragraph G
Even given these potential harms, there remain good reasons to permit homeschooling in plenty of circumstances. Parents often justifiably wish to shield their children from public schools that too often ill serve children who are at risk of bullying, or who are hurt by the culture of middle and high schools. Some children also have special abilities or needs, or simply idiosyncratic learning styles or habits, and many of these children can best or even only be educated by those who know them best.

Glossary

Qualms - Worries or fears.

Questions 27 – 33

*The text on the previous pages has 7 paragraphs **A - G**.*

Which paragraph contains the following information?

*Write your answers in boxes **27 – 33** on your answer sheet.*

27   The traditional school environment can sometimes be a good model for living in today's society.

28   Homeschooling has been accused of hindering children's social development.

29   Homeschooling can sometimes better adapt to a child's special learning needs.

30   There are companies that focus on providing homeschooling materials, guidance and curricula.

31   Homeschooling can be a financial burden for some families.

32   Homeschooling has been accused of spreading disease.

33   Homeschooling families can benefit from cheaper holidays outside the peak seasons of regular school holiday times.

Questions 34 – 37

*Choose the correct letter **A, B, C or D**.*

*Write the correct letter in boxes **34 - 37** on your answer sheet.*

34   Homeschooled children will often

    A   have no problem entering university.
    B   have difficulties with universities accepting them.
    C   have to attend universities that offer similar teaching styles to the children's childhood education experiences.
    D   not need to attend university.

35   Homeschooled children can

    A   often become bullies when they meet other children.
    B   be bullied more often.
    C   be bullied less often.
    D   be often subject to a special type of parental bullying.

36   Homeschooling classes

    A   generally take up more time than those at traditional schools.
    B   take up more or less the same time as those at traditional schools.
    C   generally take up a lot less time than those at traditional schools.
    D   generally take place in the mornings.

37   Homeschooling parents can often choose not to

    A   make their children sit exams.
    B   study certain subjects they do not favour.
    C   have any holidays away from education.
    D   share their children's results with universities.

Questions 38 – 40

Do the following statements agree with the views of the writer of the text?

*In boxes **38 - 40** on your answer sheet write:*

YES	*if the statement agrees with the writer's views*
NO	*if the statement doesn't agree with the writer's views*
NOT GIVEN	*if it is impossible to say what the writer thinks about this*

38   Many parents are challenged by the parental time required of them to homeschool their children.

39   Parents' love for their children is unconditional.

40   US law should require that parents who choose homeschooling are inspected at least once a year.

WRITING

WRITING TASK 1

You should spend about 20 minutes on this task.

The bar charts below show the prevalence of obesity among boys and girls aged 12 to 19 years by ethnicity, in the United States for the years 2004 and 2014.

Summarise the information by selecting and reporting the main features, and make comparisons where relevant.

You should write at least 150 words.

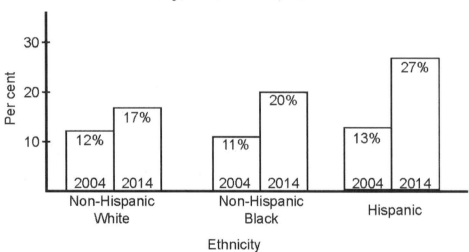

Prevalence of obesity among boys aged 12 - 19 years, by ethnicity; United States, 2004 and 2014

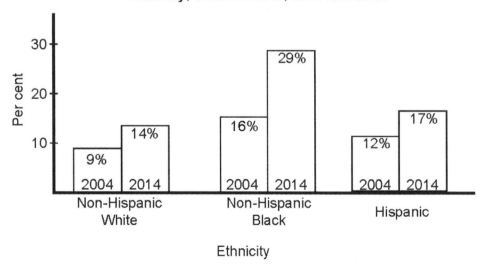

Prevalence of obesity among girls aged 12 - 19 years, by ethnicity; United States, 2004 and 2014

WRITING TASK 2

You should spend about 40 minutes on this task.

Write about the following topic:

With the improvements in today's health care, society has to care for more and more elderly people.

Do you feel that society will be able to cope with the increase in numbers of elderly people today and how can it be managed?

Give reasons for your answer and include any relevant examples from your knowledge or experience.

You should write at least 250 words.

SPEAKING

SECTION 1

- Describe one of your childhood friends.
- Did you have a lot of friends when you were young?
- Do you stay in touch with any of your childhood friends?

Topic 1   Dancing

- Do you like dancing? (Why/Why not?)
- Why do you think people dance?
- What kinds of dancing can be seen in your country?
- Do you think it's important that countries' traditional dances are preserved? (Why/Why not?)

Topic 2   Dentists

- How do you feel about visits to the dentist?
- Why do you think some people are scared of visits to the dentist?
- What are dentists like in your country?
- How have equipment and anaesthetics changed what dentistry can do?

SECTION 2

```
Describe a memorable job that you once had.
You should say:
        where this job was
        when you did this job
        what you did in this job
and briefly explain why this job was so memorable.
```

SECTION 3

Topic 1   Poverty

- What is poverty?
- What kinds of poverty exist in your country?
- What kinds of things can governments do to tackle poverty?
- How do you think poverty will change over the next 50 years?

Topic 2   Wealth

- Do you think wealth can lead to happiness?
- Is there a severe wealth gap in your country?
- Do you think it's fair that so much of the world's wealth is shared by so few people?
- Do you think the wealthy should be taxed more?

PRACTICE TEST 13

LISTENING

 Download audio recordings for the test here:
http://www.ielts-blog.com/ielts-practice-tests-downloads/

SECTION 1   Questions 1 – 10

Questions 1 – 5

Complete Happies Nursery's new child enrolment form below.

*Write **NO MORE THAN THREE WORDS AND/OR A NUMBER** from the listening for each answer.*

Happies Nursery
New Child Enrolment Form

Example	Answer
Child's age:	2

Parents' Names -   Father: Luke Beckett
                                Mother: (**1**) _____ Beckett

Address: (**2**) _____ Castle Crescent
                                                    Backley

Postcode: BA3 7TR

Telephone Numbers:

Home   Father: 01538 853 285
                      Mother: Same as father's

Mobile   Father: 07770 728 473
                      Mother: 07743 812 (**3**) _____

Work   Father: 01538 926 477
                      Mother: 01538 596 821

Fees will be paid by: (**4**) _____

Allergies: (**5**) _____

Questions 6 – 10

Complete Luke's notes for his wife below.

Use **NO MORE THAN THREE WORDS AND/OR A NUMBER** *from the listening for each answer.*

Happies Nursery – Notes

* Activities start at (**6**) _____ a.m. - parents can drop their children off after 6.30 a.m.
* From 6.30 a.m., there's a team of carers for supervision, cleaning and changing.
* All we need to bring are a sweater and some (**7**) _____ in a marked bag.

* Happies will call if Gertrude is sick - we'll have to pick her up if this happens.
* Happies is 1 mile from the County Hospital and there's always a (**8**) _____ on the premises for health supervision.

* Activities end at 4.00 p.m. (we can pick Gertrude up earlier if we want).
* Children are supervised until 6.30 p.m.
* We mustn't come after 6.30 p.m. and we should call the number in the (**9**) _____ if we're delayed.

* Happies runs a new service - supervision during the (**10**) _____. It could be useful for us sometimes.

SECTION 2   *Questions 11 – 20*

Questions 11 – 15

Complete the sentences below.

*Use **NO MORE THAN TWO WORDS AND/OR A NUMBER** from the listening for each answer.*

11   Green Trees can accommodate a maximum of _____ people.

12   Green Trees does not cater for caring for _____.

13   If residents communicate with Green Trees, they can arrange _____ to be prepared.

14   Green Trees tries to combine care and nursing with opportunities for residents to remain as _____ as possible.

15   Green Trees' fees can be found in their leaflets or on the _____.

Questions 16 – 20

Complete the table below.

Write **NO MORE THAN TWO WORDS AND/OR A NUMBER** *from the listening for each answer.*

Green Trees Old Age Centre		
What	**When**	**Notes**
Games Room Activities	Twice weekly	* Cards, bingo etc. * A (**16**) _____ is permitted to be invited - residents can meet new people
Puzzle Sessions	Regular	* Crosswords, sudoku etc.
Telling Life Stories	Not mentioned	* Sometimes not easy, but brings back lost memories * Can be recorded or written down * Good for the younger generation
All these above activities promote good condition in the (**17**) _____ and lead to all sorts of other benefits.		
Trips Away	Regular	* Trips to various places, including shows, markets and places of interest * Only (**18**) _____ trips arranged to prevent resident fatigue * Residents' families can take residents away for overnight trips - inform Green Trees when this happens
Gardening	Suitable weather	* Very fulfilling * Caring for plants helps combat sense of (**19**) _____ and makes residents feel in control * Very popular activity * Can be dangerous, but training and (**20**) _____ are provided * Supervised by the two gardeners

SECTION 3   *Questions 21 – 30*

Questions 21 – 25

*Choose the correct letter **A, B, or C**.*

21   Lily's engineering placement will be working

    A   with planes.
    B   on a bridge.
    C   in an office.

22   Ross' engineering placement will be

    A   in his family's firm.
    B   with the local government.
    C   on an oil rig.

23   Derek was refused an engineering placement in the Antarctic, because

    A   of the extreme cold.
    B   his father had to go to hospital.
    C   of a previous health problem.

24   Tanya's engineering placement will involve working with her

    A   tutor's contacts.
    B   cousin.
    C   boyfriend.

25   The students must send their engineering placement notifications to their department

    A   verbally.
    B   by email.
    C   by hand.

Questions 26 – 28

Complete the diagram below on the gas drilling station where Tanya will do her engineering placement.

Write **NO MORE THAN TWO WORDS** from the listening for each answer.

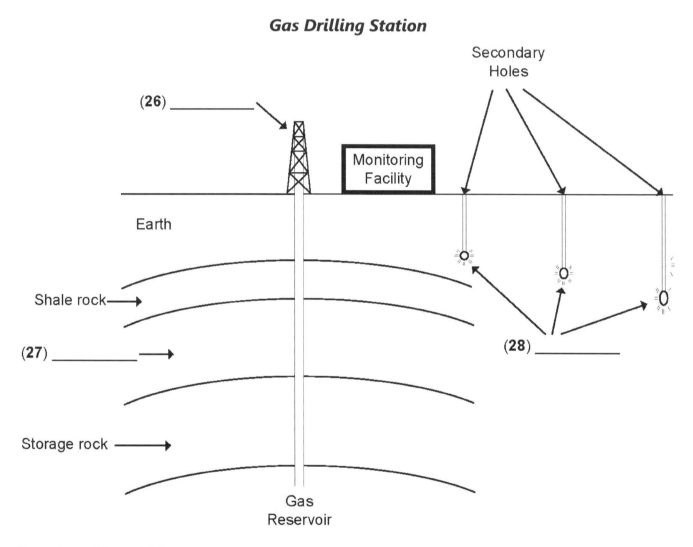

Gas Drilling Station

Questions 29 and 30

Answer the questions below. Use **NO MORE THAN TWO WORDS AND/OR A NUMBER** from the listening for each answer.

29   How will Tanya's team in the desert be in contact with their head office?

30   How long will Tanya spend in the desert at any one time?

SECTION 4   Questions 31 – 40

Questions 31 – 37

Complete the summary below on the lecture on hypnosis, hypnotism and hypnotherapy.

*Write **NO MORE THAN TWO WORDS** from the listening for each answer.*

Hypnosis, Hypnotism and Hypnotherapy

Definitions

<u>Hypnosis</u> - a different psychological state of consciousness with increased potential for (**31**) _____ .

<u>Hypnotism</u> - the study of hypnosis or the study of using suggestion during hypnosis.

<u>Hypnotherapy</u> - a therapy conducted mainly during hypnosis.

Discussion

Hypnosis creates such relaxation that certain suggestions may be made to the (**32**) _____ , bypassing the awake and logical part of the brain, so that therapy is possible. The hypnotic trance allows increased (**33**) _____ to create beneficial changes. Usually the hypnotic trance is medium, which slows certain body functions, while the brain creates alpha waves. This condition is different to normal states of consciousness, as alpha waves signify a special (**34**) _____ .

Not yet fully understood, a favoured theory is that hypnosis influences how people pay attention, which happens in the brain stem's ascending reticular formation. This area receives stimuli from the (**35**) _____ and passes on messages to the rest of the brain. Hypnosis may inhibit this area, creating great calm.

Hypnotherapy works by exploring the subconscious, where people have unrealised problems, self images, strengths and knowledge. Using hypnotherapy can exploit people's unknown (**36**) _____ and help solve problems. Many techniques are used by the hypnotherapist in the hypnotic trance. Some hypnotherapy requires little change in a patient, but more complicated behaviours require deeper therapy and psychological (**37**) _____ .

Questions 38 - 40

Choose **THREE** letters, **A** - **G**.

According to the listening, why has hypnotherapy been criticised?

A   Because any practitioners are not properly qualified.

B   Because not enough research has been done to back up the results.

C   Because the relationship between hypnotherapy and improved patient results is not easy to prove.

D   Because current tests do not use a big enough sample of the population.

E   Because some tests have shown that hypnotherapy has only had an effect because the patients thought it would.

F   Because patients give positive responses when questioned in tests because they think they ought to.

G   Because of ignorance of hypnotherapy in the critics.

READING

READING PASSAGE 1

*You should spend about 20 minutes on **Questions 1 - 13**, which are based on Reading Passage 1 below.*

The Great Fire of London

Paragraph A
The Great Fire of London swept through London in September 1666, devastating many buildings, including 13,200 houses and 87 parish churches. The Royal Exchange, the Guildhall and St. Paul's Cathedral, all built during the Middle Ages, were also all totally destroyed. Although the verified death toll was only six people, it is unknown how many people died in the Great Fire of London, because many more died through indirect causes. The financial losses caused by the fire were estimated to be £10 million, at a time when London's annual income was only £12,000. Many people were financially ruined and debtors' prisons became over-crowded.

Paragraph B
The Great Fire of London started on Sunday, 2 September 1666 in a baker's shop in Pudding Lane, belonging to Thomas Farynor. Although he claimed to have extinguished the fire, three hours later, at 1 a.m., his house was a blazing inferno. It is not certain how the fire actually began, but it is likely that it may have been caused by a spark from Farynor's oven falling onto a pile of fuel nearby. In 1979, archaeologists excavated the remains of a burnt out shop on Pudding Lane that was very close to the bakery where the fire started. In the cellar, they found the charred remnants of 20 barrels of pitch. Pitch burns very easily and would have helped to spread the fire.

Paragraph C
The fire spread quickly down Pudding Lane and carried on down Fish Hill and towards the Thames. The fire continued to spread rapidly, helped by a strong wind from the east. When it reached the Thames, it hit warehouses that were stocked with combustible products, such as oil and rope. Fortunately, the fire could not spread south of the river, because a previous blaze in 1633 had already wrecked a section of London Bridge. As the fire was spreading so quickly, most Londoners concentrated on escaping rather than fighting the fire.

Paragraph D
In the 17th century, people were not as aware of the dangers of fire as they are today. Buildings were made of timber covered in pitch and tightly packed together. The design of buildings meant flames could easily spread from building to building. Following a long, dry summer, the city was suffering a drought; water was scarce and the wooden houses had dried out, making them easier to burn.

Paragraph E

Samuel Pepys, a diarist of the period and Clerk to the Royal Navy, observed the fire and recommended to the King that buildings should be pulled down, as it could be the only way to stop the fire. The Mayor made the order to pull down burning houses using fire hooks, but the fire continued to spread. Pepys then spoke to the Admiral of the Navy and they agreed that they should blow up houses in the path of the fire. The hope was that by doing this, they would create a space to stop the fire spreading from house to house. The Navy carried out the request and by the next morning, the fire has been successfully stopped.

Paragraph F

London had to be almost totally reconstructed and many people went to the fields outside London. They stayed there for many days, sheltering in tents and shacks and some people were forced to live in this way for months and even years. Throughout 1667, people cleared rubble and surveyed the burnt area. Much time was spent planning new street layouts and drawing up new building regulations. Public buildings were paid for with money from a new coal tax, but by the end of the year only 150 new houses had been built. The new regulations were designed to prevent such a disaster happening again. Houses now had to be faced in brick instead of wood. Some streets were widened and two new streets were created. Pavements and new sewers were laid, and London's quaysides were improved. Initially, however, only temporary buildings were erected that were ill-equipped, and this enabled the plague, which was common in London at that time, to spread easily. Many people died from this and the harsh winter that followed the fire.

Paragraph G

In 1666, there was no organised fire brigade. Fire fighting was very basic with little skill or knowledge involved. Leather buckets, axes and water squirts were used to fight the fire, but they had little effect. As a result of the Great Fire of London, early fire brigades were formed by insurance companies. Building insurance was very profitable and many more insurance companies were set up, establishing their own fire brigades. These brigades were sent to insured properties if a fire occurred to minimise damage and cost. Firemarks were used to identify - and advertise - different insurance companies. They were placed on the outside of an insured building and brigades would use them to determine whether a building was insured by them. If a building was on fire, several brigades would attend. If they did not see their specific firemark attached to the building, they would leave the property to burn. Some old firemarks can still be seen on London buildings today. Also, fire fighters wore brightly coloured uniforms to distinguish themselves from rival insurance brigades. Although this was a step in the right direction, fire fighters received little training and the equipment used remained very basic.

Glossary

Pitch – A thick liquid made from petroleum or coal tar.

Questions 1 – 7

*The text on the previous pages has 7 paragraphs (**A – G**).*

Choose the correct heading for each paragraph from the list of headings below.

*Write the correct number (**i – x**) in boxes **1 – 7** on your answer sheet.*

i	Vulnerable Buildings
ii	The Effect on Trade
iii	How it Started
iv	A Positive from the Ashes
v	Food Shortages
vi	The Movement of the Fire
vii	The Effects of the Smoke
viii	Extinguishing the Fire
ix	The Costs
x	A New London

1	Paragraph A
2	Paragraph B
3	Paragraph C
4	Paragraph D
5	Paragraph E
6	Paragraph F
7	Paragraph G

Questions 8 – 11

Choose **FOUR** letters, **A - G**.

What **FOUR** of the following were effects of the Great Fire of London?

Write the correct letter, **A - G**, in any order in boxes **8 - 11** on your answer sheet.

A   Officially, only six people died.

B   The French economy benefitted from the destruction of businesses in London.

C   Some people had to live rough in fields for years following the fire.

D   The English royal family were forced to live outside London for 18 months.

E   Disease spread more easily.

F   An enquiry was completed by the government into why the damage was so bad.

G   Fire fighting services were launched.

Questions 12 and 13

Complete the sentences below.

Write **NO MORE THAN THREE WORDS** from the text for each answer.

Write your answers in boxes **12 and 13** on your answer sheet.

12   One measure to prevent further fires was to ensure that London houses would have _____ facades in the future.

13   People could differentiate the fire brigades from different insurance companies by their _____.

READING PASSAGE 2

You should spend about 20 minutes on **Questions 14 - 26**, which are based on Reading Passage 2 below.

A New Threat in Yellowstone

It has long been known that Yellowstone National Park lies over an enormous supervolcano. The term 'supervolcano' implies a volcanic centre that has had an eruption of magnitude 8 on the Volcano Explosivity Index (VEI), meaning the measured deposits for that eruption are greater than 1,000 cubic kilometres. This sounds worrying and Professor George Peters details the possible results if something were to happen. "A major eruption would obliterate the surroundings within a radius of hundreds of kilometres, and cover the rest of the United States and Canada with multiple inches of ash. This would shut down agriculture and cause global climate cooling for as long as a decade." To calm everyone down, geologist, Tony Masters, explains there is little to fear today. "All VEI 8 eruptions, including the last at Yellowstone, occurred tens of thousands to millions of years ago. Another eruption could occur, but it is very unlikely to happen in the next million years or so."

Yellowstone is no stranger to controversy. There was a previous media accusation that US Geological Survey (USGS) geologists had not done their work properly and that the identification of Yellowstone as a supervolcano was not done until scientists looked at photographs of Yellowstone from space. The Yellowstone scientists denied this. Spokesman Alice Wheeler clarifies their position. "The scientist who first identified the three Yellowstone calderas was from the USGS and he told the world about the great eruptions that formed them. He traced out the caldera boundaries through old fashioned field work, walking around with a hammer and hand lens and looking carefully at the rocks and their distributions." The National Aeronautics and Space Administration (NASA) also agreed. Stan Forsyth, their spokesman, explains. "Several authors have written that these large calderas in Yellowstone were discovered from space, but we suspect that the rumour probably got started because initial field work that identified them was partly funded by NASA."

A new problem in Yellowstone is that the supervolcano has now been discovered to be larger than originally thought and this has made people feel more nervous. Seismologists at the University of Utah have worked with several other institutions to create an image of the Yellowstone magma reservoir using a technique called seismic tomography. Masters student, Julia Grey, explains the results. "By looking closely at data from thousands of earthquakes, we have discovered that there are two magma reservoirs, one shallow and one deep, and that they are much larger than originally believed. The shallow one was previously known about to us, but the deeper one is a new finding."

To create an image of this second magma reservoir beneath Yellowstone, the research teams reviewed data from thousands of earthquakes. Seismic waves travel slower through hot, partially molten rock and faster in cold, solid rock. The researchers made a map of the locations where seismic waves travel more slowly, which provided a sub-surface image of the hot or partially molten bodies in the crust beneath Yellowstone. The deeper magma storage region extends from 20 to 50 kilometres depth, contains about 2 per cent melt, and is about 4.5 times larger than the shallow magma body. The shallower magma storage region is about 90 kilometres long, extends from 5 to 17 kilometres depth, and is 2.5 times larger than a prior, less accurate, study indicated. This magma reservoir contains between about 5 to 15 per cent molten rock. Although this is the crustal magma storage region that has fuelled Yellowstone's past volcanic activity, magma typically does not erupt unless it has greater than 50 per cent melt.

The US and world media were quick to dramatise the finding and exaggerate the threat that these findings represent. Yellowstone park scientist, Amy Brent, has calming words. "These findings do not increase the assessment of volcanic hazard for Yellowstone. The inferred magma storage region is no larger than we already knew. The research simply makes a better image of the magmatic system. Simply, we have more key information about how the Yellowstone volcano works."

Many independent reports back up Brent's comments and have shown that the Yellowstone area has been on a long cycle of periodic eruptions. Eruptions are extremely infrequent in supervolcanos, and eventually the cycle ends in their deaths. US government geologist, Andrea Haller, explains the state of the Yellowstone supervolcano. "By investigating the patterns of behaviour in two previously completed caldera cycles, we can suggest that the current activity of Yellowstone is on the dying cycle." This is based on comparisons with other supervolcanos. Scientists know the behaviour of the past and they know at what comparative stage Yellowstone is right now. It is believed that Yellowstone is currently on a third and dying cycle. This can be concluded by the fact that dying volcanos produce less fresh molten material from the Earth's crust. Haller continues. "We've observed a lot of material in the magma chambers that represent recycled volcanic rocks, which were once buried inside of calderas and are now getting reused. Yellowstone has erupted enough of this material already to suggest that the future melting potential of the crust is getting exhausted."

Whatever the truth about Yellowstone, it seems that during the lives of most people, the geological status of Yellowstone can still prove hazardous. The park has often been closed due to volcanic activity in the past and this is likely to happen again before the volcano becomes harmless.

Glossary

Caldera – an enormous volcano crater.

Magma – melted rock.

Questions 14 – 20

Look at the following statements (questions 14 - 20) and the list of people below.

Match each statement with the correct person's initials.

Write the correct initials in boxes 14 - 20 on your answer sheet.

14   The Yellowstone volcano is on its dying supervolcano cycle.

15   The Yellowstone supervolcano was first identified by traditional geology work.

16   A major Yellowstone eruption would cause Canadian farming to cease.

17   The Yellowstone magma chambers are larger than previously thought.

18   A major Yellowstone eruption last occurred thousands of years ago.

19   Scientists now know better about the functioning of the Yellowstone volcano.

20   NASA has provided money in the past to help research on the Yellowstone supervolcano.

GP	George Peters
TM	Tony Masters
AW	Alice Wheeler
SF	Stan Forsyth
JG	Julia Grey
AB	Amy Brent
AH	Andrea Haller

Questions 21 – 23

Label the diagram below.

*Write **NO MORE THAN THREE WORDS AND/OR A NUMBER** from the text for each answer.*

*Write your answers in boxes **21 - 23** on your answer sheet.*

The Yellowstone Supervolcano

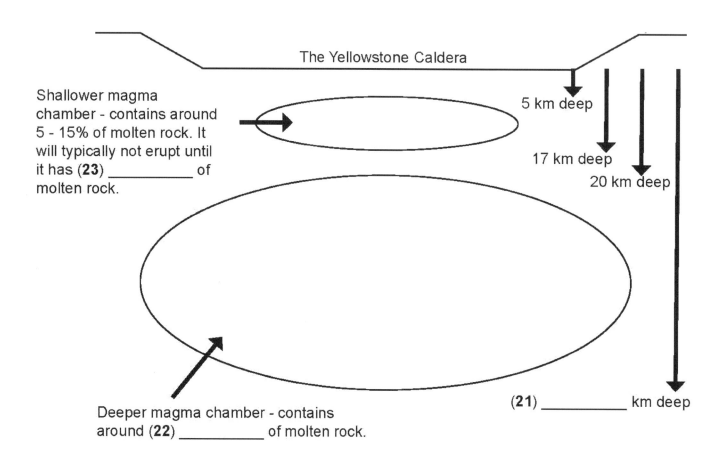

The Yellowstone Caldera

Shallower magma chamber - contains around 5 - 15% of molten rock. It will typically not erupt until it has (**23**) _____ of molten rock.

5 km deep

17 km deep

20 km deep

Deeper magma chamber - contains around (**22**) _____ of molten rock.

(**21**) _____ km deep

Questions 24 – 26

Choose the correct letter *A, B, C or D*.

Write the correct letter in boxes *24 - 26* on your answer sheet.

24   Images of the magma chambers can be made, because

    A   of the different speeds that seismic waves travel through different states of rock.
    B   seismic waves cannot penetrate any sections of magma.
    C   seismic waves only detect colder rock.
    D   seismic waves travel very fast.

25   The death of the Yellowstone supervolcano

    A   will occur in the next few years.
    B   cannot ever be predicted.
    C   can be probably predicted due to the lack of fresh molten rock.
    D   will follow the next major eruption.

26   The Yellowstone National Park

    A   will probably have to be closed at certain times of danger.
    B   will probably never open again due to the dangers.
    C   will never need to be closed in the lifetimes of people today.
    D   will stop wild animals entering it if possible.

READING PASSAGE 3

*You should spend about 20 minutes on **Questions 27 - 40**, which are based on Reading Passage 3 below.*

The Psychology of Wealth

What stops people from succeeding financially and having on-going prosperity in their life? The answer is generally focused around the belief that financial success is not a possibility. There are many people who have unconscious barriers that prevent them from having the wealth and abundance that they deserve.

At a conscious level, most people think they are doing everything possible to achieve their goals. However, there still might be some unwitting part of them that does not believe they can obtain success. The more that unconscious part is avoided, the more a person will be blocked in their everyday life. Another problem is that, instead of focusing on all the possible ways to get rich, many people have an obsession about what they do not have. An interesting pattern develops in which they can become angry or resentful over their situation and this in turn can limit these people in their lives more and more. Individuals would find it so much easier to get ahead in life with a peaceful state of mind, rather than an angry or resentful one.

A first step in understanding the unconscious patterning of a person's financial situation is to explore the deeper nature of how they represent money. For example, a person with money issues may have had parents who lived in poverty, and they subsequently formed a 'Depression Era' mentality. An unconscious belief can develop that he or she will always have to struggle financially, because that is what their parents did. Alternatively, the person might have had a parent tell them over and over again that they will never be successful, and eventually they begin to believe it.

It is very common for children to unconsciously form limiting beliefs around money at an early age. In the field of Neuro Linguistic Programming (NLP), these types of limiting beliefs are referred to as 'imprints.' An imprint is basically a memory that is formed at an early age, and can serve as a root for both the limiting and empowering beliefs that people form as children. Some of the beliefs that people may develop at early ages are not always healthy, and are created as a result of a traumatic or confusing experience that they have forgotten. How we unconsciously and consciously view the world in terms of money is often based on such beliefs.

A primary and fundamental psychological difference between those who do well financially and those who do not revolves around beliefs. For example, many people do not even view financial success as an option. They do not have the capability to open themselves up to all of the possibilities that are available for achieving prosperity and they will nearly always get stuck in a monthly routine, so that they are unwilling to take risks or try something different, because they are afraid that they will end up being even worse off than before.

Another issue can be that people become over-absorbed with the idea of making money and this can be extremely unhealthy. Money does not determine who you are; it's simply a resource. There is a term called 'affluenza,' which has been defined as "a painful, contagious, socially transmitted condition of overload, debt, anxiety and waste resulting from the dogged pursuit of more." Affluenza is an unsustainable and seriously unhealthy addiction to personal and societal economic growth. It is most acute in those who inherit wealth and seem to have no purpose or direction. For those with wealth or for those who desire it more than anything, abandoning the urge for more can often be the key to being more successful, and certainly happier. Once people stop equating their self-worth with money, then the doors of possibility can swing open for them, because they are willing to try more things. Once they start feeling better about themselves, they become less fearful and can be open to trying something completely different.

So, can money make people happy? Research shows that it does up to a point, after which there are diminishing returns, so that the extremely wealthy are no happier than the comfortably well off. Rich nations are generally happier than poor ones, but the relationship is far from consistent; other factors like political stability, freedom and security also play a part. Research likewise shows that the money-happiness connection seems to be stronger for people paid hourly than those on a salary. This is presumably because salaried people can more easily compensate with career satisfaction. Money can also impair the ability to enjoy the simple things in life, which rather offsets the happiness that wealth brings.

Money can also impair people's satisfaction in their play and humanitarian works. When someone has done something out of the goodness of their heart, they can be insulted by offers of payment. Cognitive dissonance experiments show that paying people derisory amounts of money for their work results in them enjoying it less and doing it less well than if they had no pay at all. The capacity for monetary reward to undermine a person's intrinsic pleasure in work performance has been demonstrated neurologically.

In conclusion, people need to realise that their own attitudes to wealth can affect their chances of acquiring both money and happiness. As a person begins to embrace self worth and open himself or herself up to the idea of what is possible, he or she will attract wealth and prosperity into their life. The outer world is truly a reflection of people's inner worlds. If someone feels good inside, generally it will show on the outside and they will draw positive experiences into their life.

Questions 27 – 29

Complete the notes below.

Write **NO MORE THAN TWO WORDS** for each answer.

Write your answers in boxes **27 - 29** on your answer sheet.

---

* Some people unwittingly reject the prospect of becoming rich; these (**27**) _____ stop them from financial success.
* Most people believe they do the best they can, but sometimes they don't really believe in their potential.
* If people do not face up to this lack of self-belief, they'll encounter more and more obstacles.
* People can also have an (**28**) _____ about their lack of possessions.
* Anger is a result, which hinders their progress as well.
* People whose parents were poor may feel they will also be poor.
* A (**29**) _____ who is always negative about a child's prospects may also be eventually believed.

Questions 30 – 34

Do the following statements agree with the views of the writer of the text?

In boxes **30 - 34** on your answer sheet write:

YES	if the statement agrees with the writer's views
NO	if the statement doesn't agree with the writer's views
NOT GIVEN	if it is impossible to say what the writer thinks about this

30   A person can develop unhelpful imprints about money when a child.

31   Although important, belief is not a key part of whether someone can become financially successful.

32   Those people stuck in a monthly routine are the most likely to try something different.

33   The problem of 'affluenza' has been in the media a lot recently.

34   'Affluenza' is more common in people who have not had to work for their money.

Questions 35 – 40

Complete the summary below.

*Write **NO MORE THAN THREE WORDS** from the text for each answer.*

*Write your answers in boxes **35 - 40** on your answer sheet.*

Money and Happiness

(**35**) _____ mean people are not happier with wealth beyond a certain amount. Rich countries are happier than poor ones, but this is simplistic, due to other relevant (**36**) _____. Salaried workers have been shown to be happier than wage-paid workers, maybe due to (**37**) _____. Rich people also sometimes do not enjoy life's (**38**) _____.

Money can also relate to how people approach doing things and (**39**) _____ have proved this. The complex relationship between a (**40**) _____ and enjoyment of work has also been proved.

Changing their attitudes to wealth can make some people happier and allow them to acquire money more easily.

WRITING

WRITING TASK 1

You should spend about 20 minutes on this task.

The graph below shows the annual visitor spend for visitors to New Zealand from 5 countries for the years 1996 to 2014.

Summarise the information by selecting and reporting the main features, and make comparisons where relevant.

You should write at least 150 words.

Annual Visitor Spending in New Zealand; 1996 – 2014
Australia; USA; UK; Japan; China

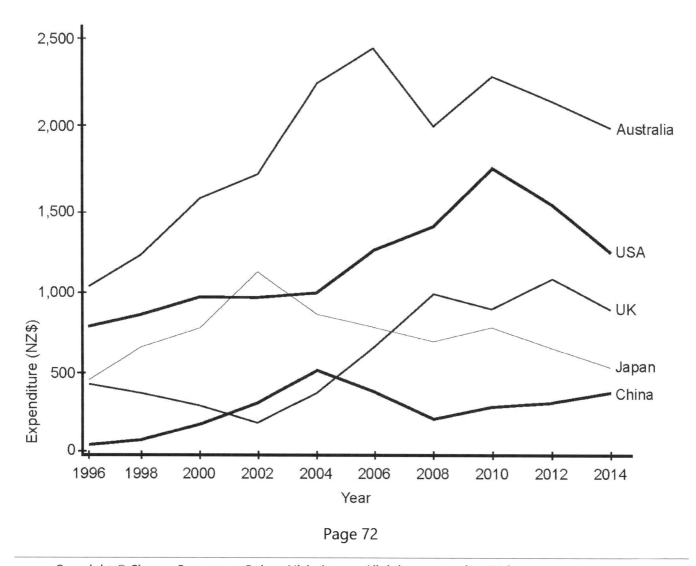

WRITING TASK 2

You should spend about 40 minutes on this task.

Write about the following topic:

Traffic on roads has become a problem in nearly every country in the world.

What can be done to reduce the amount of traffic at a society level and at an individual level?

Give reasons for your answer and include any relevant examples from your knowledge or experience.

You should write at least 250 words.

SPEAKING

SECTION 1

- Describe the street where you grew up when you were young.
- Was there a good community spirit where you grew up?
- What kinds of things do you remember about your neighbours from where you grew up?

Topic 1   Shopping
- Who does the grocery shopping in your household?
- Do you prefer a supermarket or visiting markets and smaller shops? (Why?)
- Do you like to shop online? (Why/Why not?)
- What are your feelings about people who are addicted to shopping?

Topic 2   Immigration
- Does your country experience much immigration and emigration? (Why/Why not?)
- How is immigration helpful to a country?
- What things should immigrants know before they move to another country?
- Do you think countries should drop all restrictions on immigration? (Why/Why not?)

SECTION 2

> Describe a well-known building in your country that you like.
> You should say:
>> where this building is
>> what the function of the building is
>> what people think about the building
> and explain why you like this building.

SECTION 3

Topic 1   Architecture
- What do you think about your country's old and modern styles of architecture?
- What do you feel about the increase of people living in apartment blocks?
- What are some of the factors that affect architectural decisions?
- How do you think your country's architecture will change over the next 50 years?

Topic 2   Preserving Old Buildings
- What are the most significant old buildings and monuments in your country?
- Do you prefer old buildings or new buildings? (Why?)
- How important is it to preserve national monuments and famous buildings?
- Do you think people should be able to visit monuments and famous buildings for free or should they pay? (Why?)

PRACTICE TEST 14

LISTENING

Download audio recordings for the test here:
http://www.ielts-blog.com/ielts-practice-tests-downloads/

SECTION 1   *Questions 1 – 10*

Questions 1 – 6

Complete Mrs. Davis' notes below.

Write **NO MORE THAN THREE WORDS AND/OR A NUMBER** *from the listening for each answer.*

Dominic's Summer Sports Camp

Example	*Answer*
Dominic can join a group for children between 11 and ____13____ years. This won't have children too old for him.	

The sports coaching is done by sports science students, who are supervised by
(**1**) _____ with more experience. All staff have an enhanced police check and company training. They are also trained in (**2**) _____ and there's a hospital nearby.

Dominic will need warm clothing and changes of clothing in case of bad weather. If weather is bad, everyone will move into the (**3**) _____ of Wentmount School.

Sessions   Morning, afternoon or both. Dominic can do both and make some new
            friends.

Food   Give Dominic a packed lunch or he can join the group lunches.
            Group Lunches - Basic starter; hot main course; (**4**) _____ to finish with.

Dominic will need his sports equipment that he wants to bring and some (**5**) _____ for between meals.

Timings   Morning Session   9.30 a.m. - 12.00 midday
            Afternoon Session 1.30 p.m. - (**6**) _____ p.m.

Children must be picked up by 5 p.m.

Questions 7 – 10

*Choose the correct letter **A, B, or C**.*

7 Dominic's favourite sport is

    A   cricket.
    B   swimming.
    C   football.

8 Mrs. Davis says that the instructors should know that

    A   Dominic's legs are weak.
    B   Dominic will have to go to hospital at the start of the summer.
    C   Dominic broke his arm during the winter.

9 The first week of the camp, Dominic will

    A   be picked up by his mother.
    B   go home by bus.
    C   walk home with friends.

10 To keep Dominic's reserved place on the sports camp, Mrs. Davis has to return the form

    A   within two weeks.
    B   the next day.
    C   within a week.

SECTION 2   *Questions 11 – 20*

Questions 11 – 15

*Match the situation given (questions **11 - 15**) with the advice given in the listening by Police Constable Dawson (**A - I**).*

*Write the correct letter (**A - I**) next to questions **11 - 15**.*

11   Your bicycle has been stolen.   _____

12   You are worried that someone is following you.   _____

13   You've bought a car.   _____

14   Your house is broken into, but your bank cards are not taken.   _____

15   You need to throw away some documents that have sensitive information. _____

A	Cancel your bank cards.
B	Establish a security routine.
C	Find a secure storage place for your bank cards.
D	Go to a nearby shop and explain what has happened.
E	Make sure a photo and description goes to the police.
F	Hide behind a nearby car.
G	Burn them.
H	Buy a paper shredder.
I	Search the nearby area.

Questions 16 – 20

Complete the sentences below.

*Use **NO MORE THAN TWO WORDS** from the listening for each answer.*

16   _____ is what allows cell phone thieves to succeed.

17   Pickpockets like stealing in busy _____, so be extra aware in these places.

18   People leaving subway stations often have their cell phones stolen when they look to see if they have a _____.

19   People should consult their _____ to find out how to switch on the security features available on their cell phones.

20   If your cell phone is stolen, the police have to know more than its _____ and colour if they are to get it back to you.

SECTION 3   *Questions 21 – 30*

Questions 21 – 25

Complete the summary below on the Kenyan flower industry.

*Write **NO MORE THAN TWO WORDS** from the listening for each answer.*

The Kenyan Flower Industry

The Kenyan flower industry is Kenya's largest after (**21**) _____ and tea and has increased by 31% over the last 5 years. Originally started to contribute to British East Africa's (**22**) _____, it continued to flourish after independence due to its geographical position and variety of climate conditions.

Economic advantages, such as beneficial (**23**) _____ have kept costs low and good logistics have been set up to service world flower markets. Labour and energy costs are also low and there is no (**24**) _____ on European exports from Kenya.

Floriculture is Kenya's 2nd highest foreign exchange earner and it generates plenty of (**25**) _____ for Kenya's public economy - 50,000 to 70,000 people are employed directly and 1½ million people indirectly.

Questions 26 – 30

Complete the table below on problems and criticisms of the Kenyan flower industry.

Write **NO MORE THAN TWO WORDS** from the listening for each answer.

Problems and Criticisms	
Workforce Disputes	* Not wholly resolved yet
High Oil Prices	* Increased (**26**) _____ costs
Heavy Rains + Extended Drought	* Affected the crop size
Competition	* Mostly from countries on or near the equator * Biggest competitors - The Netherlands, Colombia, Ecuador and Ethiopia * Competition getting fiercer due to the numbers of roses produced and better (**27**) _____ from the competition.
Sustainability	* Wages are often too low - workers have a problem with poor disposable income * Trade unions are discouraged
Water Usage	* 1 rose's water footprint is 7 - 13 litres * There has been a very large water export within the flowers out of the country * Lakes have declined in level and (**28**) _____
Pollution	* In local lakes * Large producers initially blamed, but it's now proved that small holders are also to blame * The nutrient load in lakes is too high * Attempts at improvement by increasing the price of (**29**) _____ and other regulatory measures - political and tribal issues have resisted these attempted efforts
Outdated Farm Methods	* Improving situation * More organic ways of (**30**) _____ are being used * More water recycling and waste disposal systems in participating farms have led to long-term costs savings

SECTION 4　　　Questions 31 – 40

Questions 31 – 37

Complete the flow chart that summarises the cotton growing process.

*Use **NO MORE THAN TWO WORDS** from the listening for each answer.*

Growing Cotton

Planting - seeds planted at a fixed depths and **(31)** _____. Seedlings sprout after around a week or two, depending on temperature and moisture.

↓

Weed Control - weeds can affect yields. Addressed with close cultivation and seeds planted deep into **(32)** _____ - weeds high and dry. Herbicides are also used.

↓

Insect Management - Insects can destroy the crop - some plants compensate by producing more **(33)** _____. The plants are protected by evaluated chemicals and modern biotechnology.

↓

Irrigation - Cotton very efficient with water: cotton generates more **(34)** _____ for 1 gallon of water than other US crops. US cotton depends on rain, although supplemental irrigation has increased to deal with drought and problem yields.

↓

Harvesting - This must be done before bad weather comes. It's done by **(35)** _____ in the US - stripper harvesters and spindle pickers used.

↓

Ginning - separates lint from seeds. Cotton then dried and sent to a warehouse.

↓

Storage - After quality assessment, cotton sold or stored. If stored in a government-approved warehouse, it can be used as security for a **(36)** _____.

↓

Cottonseed - byproduct from the cotton crop. Used as salad oil or high **(37)** _____ animal feed.

Questions 38 – 40

Complete the diagram below of the three nozzle positions for crop-spraying cotton.

Write **NO MORE THAN THREE WORDS** from the listening for each answer.

Three Nozzle Positions for Crop-spraying Cotton

1

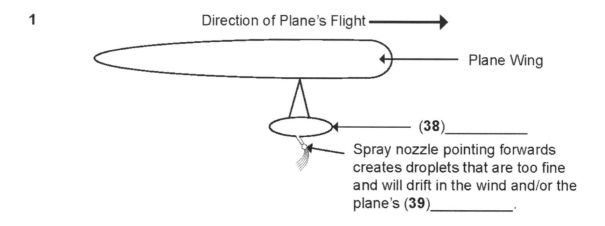

Direction of Plane's Flight ➔

Plane Wing

(38)_____

Spray nozzle pointing forwards creates droplets that are too fine and will drift in the wind and/or the plane's (39)_____.

2

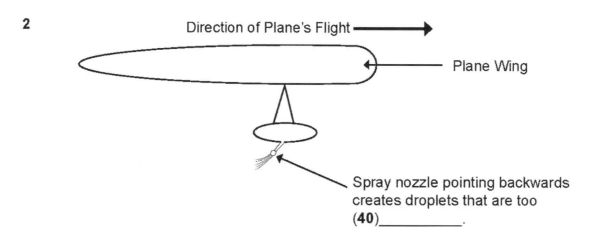

Direction of Plane's Flight ➔

Plane Wing

Spray nozzle pointing backwards creates droplets that are too (40)_____.

3

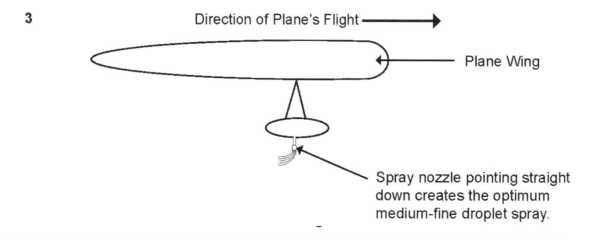

Direction of Plane's Flight ➔

Plane Wing

Spray nozzle pointing straight down creates the optimum medium-fine droplet spray.

READING

READING PASSAGE 1

*You should spend about 20 minutes on **Questions 1 - 13**, which are based on Reading Passage 1 below.*

Braille

Paragraph A
Braille is a system of touch reading and writing for blind persons in which raised dots represent the letters of the alphabet. Braille also contains equivalents for punctuation marks and provides symbols to show letter groupings. Braille is read by moving the hand or hands from left to right along each line. Both hands are usually involved in the reading process, and reading is generally done with the index fingers. The average reading speed is about 125 words per minute, but greater speeds of up to 200 words per minute are possible.

Paragraph B
The history of Braille goes all the way back to the early 1800's, when Charles Berbier developed a unique system known as 'night writing,' so that soldiers could communicate safely during the night. Being a military veteran, Berbier had seen several soldiers killed, because they used lamps after dark to read combat messages. The light shining from the lamps told the enemy where the French soldiers were and this inevitably led to the loss of many men. Berbier based his night writing system on a raised 12-dot cell; two dots wide and six dots tall. Each dot or combination of dots within the cell denoted a letter or a phonetic sound. The problem with the military code was that the human fingertip could not feel all the dots with one touch.

Paragraph C
Louis Braille was born January 4, 1809, in a small village near Paris. His father, a leather worker, often used sharp tools in his work. While playing in his father's shop when he was three, Louis injured his eye with an awl. In spite of good care, infection set in and soon left him completely blind. At eleven years old, Braille was inspired to modify Charles Berbier's night writing code in an effort to create an efficient written communication system for fellow blind individuals. One year earlier, he had enrolled at the National Institute of the Blind in Paris and he spent the next nine years developing and refining the system of raised dots that has come to be known by his name, Braille.

Paragraph D
Braille's code was based on cells with only six dots, instead of 12, as in Berbier's. This improvement was crucial, because it meant that a fingertip could encompass the entire cell unit with one impression and move rapidly from one cell to the next. Over time, Braille gradually came to be accepted throughout the world as the fundamental form of written communication for blind individuals, and today it remains basically as he invented it. There have, however, been some small modifications to the Braille

system. Partly because of the size that Braille pages occupy, and partly to improve the speed of writing and reading, the literary Braille codes for English and many other languages employ contractions that substitute shorter sequences for the full spelling of commonly occurring letter groups. For example, 'the' is usually just one character in Braille. The use of contractions permits faster Braille reading and helps reduce the size of Braille books, making them much less cumbersome. Braille passed away in 1853 at the age of 43, a year before his home country of France adopted Braille as its official communication system for blind individuals. A few years later in 1860, Braille made its way to America, where it was adopted by many institutions.

Paragraph E

A modern application of Braille is its use with computers. Reading electronic documents using hands instead of eyes may sound almost impossible, however, this is actually what many blind persons can do nowadays. This is done through a device known as a Braille display. Braille displays are hardware that enable users to read in Braille the text displayed on the computer screen. Using this, blind people can navigate through the computer's desktop, create and edit documents, and browse the Internet. Once connected to the computer, the Braille display will acquire the currently highlighted text on the screen. The screen reader will then translate the text into Braille and the Braille display will display it on its built-in Braille cells. Braille displays are refreshable, which means that when the user moves to a specific line of text, the device displays the text's Braille equivalent. Then, when the user moves to another line, the device automatically displays that new line in Braille.

Paragraph F

The Braille display is just one of the devices used by blind people in accessing the computer and other electronic hardware. Apart from this device, blind people also use synthetic speech provided by screen readers, which reads electronic text in a semi-human voice. The main difference between Braille displays and synthetic speech is that Braille displays actually let users read text content. As screen readers only let users hear the text on the screen, Braille displays are more useful for users who are both deaf and blind.

Paragraph G

Louis Braille's legacy has enlightened the lives of millions of people who are blind, and blind individuals from all over the world benefit from Braille's work daily. Today, Braille code is transcribed in many different languages worldwide. Now people who are blind can enjoy all the printed word has to offer just like everyone else. The effect is tremendously empowering and helps them achieve success in school and in their careers.

Questions 1 – 7

*The text on the previous pages has 7 paragraphs **A - G**.*

Which paragraph contains the following information?

*Write your answers in boxes **1 – 7** on your answer sheet.*

1   Braille died before his native country officially began to use Braille as their communication of choice with blind people.

2   A system previous to Braille's was too big for a single finger to read a symbol at one time.

3   Braille can be used with a variety of different languages.

4   It took Louis Braille nine years to create his reading system for the blind.

5   Braille can be used to read highlighted text on a computer.

6   Braille is able to show when punctuation is used.

7   Braille displays are better than screen readers for people who are deaf as well as blind.

Questions 8 – 13

Complete the sentences below.

*Write **NO MORE THAN TWO WORDS** from the text for each answer.*

*Write your answers in boxes **8 - 13** on your answer sheet.*

8   Braille reading is usually done by moving the hands' _____ along a line of raised dots.

9   Berbier's reading system was devised to help _____ with reading safely at night.

10   The dots in Berbier's reading system represented either a letter or a _____.

11   Louis Braille's accident with an _____ left him blind for the rest of his life.

12   Braille uses _____ that allow Braille books to be shorter than they would be otherwise.

13   A Braille display is _____ that can be used in conjunction with a computer.

READING PASSAGE 2

*You should spend about 20 minutes on **Questions 14 - 26**, which are based on Reading Passage 2 below.*

Black Holes

Black holes have been common topics in media and entertainment for some time. The actual name 'Black Hole' is misleading, as a hole implies an emptiness and a black hole is anything but empty space. A black hole is rather a great amount of matter packed into a very small area. For example, the amount of compressed matter in a black hole would be seen in a star ten times more massive than the Sun squeezed into a sphere approximately the diameter of New York City.

There are different types of black holes. A static black hole is one that is relatively simple to describe, as it does not rotate and it does not have a charge. A static black hole has three things of particular interest. The outer part is known as the photon sphere, so named as photons orbit the black hole here. Like all planets and stars, black holes have gravity, except much more than anything else. The photon sphere is the only place where light rays can have orbits around the black hole, though they are very unstable. The next point of interest is the event horizon. Like the photon sphere, this is just a mathematical distance based on gravity. Once something passes beyond the event horizon, it can never leave the black hole, as the gravitational pull is too strong. As even the light reflecting off an object will be drawn into a black hole, it is not possible to see something once it passes the event horizon. The centre of a black hole is the singularity and this where all the matter of a black hole from its origin lies, along with anything drawn in. The singularity is a difficult thing to describe. It is not a place, but more where the curvature of space time is infinite. It is not known what goes on there, but it is known that it depends on quantum mechanics.

Although the term was not coined until 1967 by Princeton physicist John Wheeler, the idea of an object in space so massive and dense that light cannot escape it has been around for centuries. Most famously, black holes were predicted by Einstein's theory of general relativity, which showed that, when a massive star dies, it leaves behind a small and dense remnant core. If the core's mass is more than about three times the mass of the Sun, Einstein's equations showed that the force of gravity overwhelms all other forces and produces a black hole.

Scientists cannot directly observe black holes with telescopes that detect X-rays, light, or other forms of electromagnetic radiation. They can, however, infer the presence of black holes and study them by detecting their effect on other matter nearby. If a black hole passes through a cloud of interstellar matter, for example, it will draw matter inward in a process known as 'accretion.' A similar process can occur if a normal star passes close to a black hole. In this case, the black hole can tear the star apart, as it pulls it toward itself. As the attracted matter accelerates and heats up, it emits X-rays that radiate into space. Recent discoveries offer some evidence that black holes have a dramatic influence on things around them, emitting powerful gamma ray bursts, absorbing nearby stars, and both stimulating and hindering the growth of new stars.

There is a good, relatively recent example of detecting a black hole from events near it. An international team of astronomers has identified a candidate for the smallest-known black hole using data from NASA's Rossi X-ray Timing Explorer (RXTE). The evidence comes from a specific type of X-ray pattern, nicknamed a 'heartbeat,' because of its resemblance to an electrocardiogram. The pattern until now has been recorded in only one other black hole system. The system in question combines a normal star with a black hole that may weigh less than three times the Sun's mass. That is, of course, near the theoretical mass boundary where black holes become possible. Gas from the normal star streams toward the black hole and forms a disk around it. Friction within the disk heats the gas to millions of degrees, which is hot enough to emit X-rays. Cyclical variations in the intensity of the X-rays observed reflect processes taking place within the gas disk. Therefore it is by observing the gas disk that scientists can predict the presence of the black hole, rather than seeing it itself, which is, of course, impossible.

Although the basic formation process is understood, one perennial mystery in the science of black holes is that they appear to exist on two radically different size scales. At the one end, there are the countless black holes that are the remnants of massive stars. Peppered throughout the Universe, these 'stellar mass' black holes are generally 10 to 24 times as massive as the Sun. Astronomers spot them when other stars draw near enough for some of the matter surrounding them to be snared by the black hole's gravity, churning out X-rays in the process. Most stellar black holes, however, lead isolated lives and are impossible to detect. Judging from the number of stars large enough to produce such black holes, however, scientists estimate that there are as many as ten million to a billion such black holes in the Milky Way alone. At the other end of the size spectrum are the giants known as 'supermassive' black holes, which are millions, if not billions, of times as massive as the Sun. Astronomers believe that supermassive black holes lie at the middle of virtually all large galaxies. Astronomers can detect them by watching for their effects on nearby stars and gas.

Questions 14 – 17

Do the following statements agree with the information given in the text?

In boxes 14 – 17 on your answer sheet write:

TRUE	*if the statement agrees with the information*
FALSE	*if the statement contradicts the information*
NOT GIVEN	*if there is no information on this*

14   Scientists' knowledge of quantum mechanics has allowed them to predict what happens in the singularity of a black hole.

15   Einstein's work theoretically showed the existence of black holes.

16   X-rays emitted from near black holes are picked up by telescopes on satellites orbiting the Earth.

17   Black holes can actually help the creation of new stars.

Questions 18 and 19

*Label the diagram below. Write **NO MORE THAN THREE WORDS** from the text for each answer. Write your answers in boxes **18 and 19** on your answer sheet.*

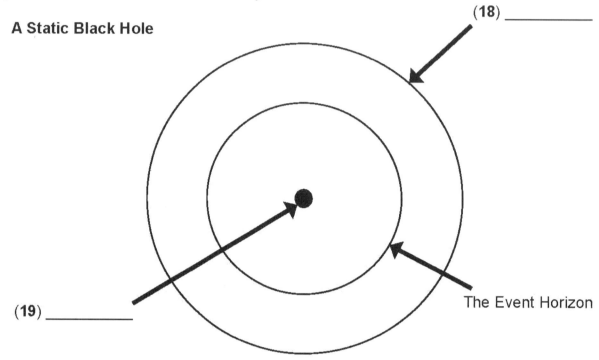

A Static Black Hole

(18) _____

(19) _____

The Event Horizon

Questions 20 – 26

*Complete the summary below. Write **NO MORE THAN THREE WORDS** from the text for each answer. Write your answers in boxes **20 - 26** on your answer sheet.*

Small and Large Black Holes

The smallest black hole ever found has been discovered with an X-ray pattern similar to an (**20**) _____. It is only just the right (**21**) _____ to have become a black hole. It was spotted when gas from a nearby sun encircled it in a (**22**) _____ shape. The super-heated gas displays (**23**) _____ in its emitted X-rays that reflect what is happening.

Black holes either seem to be very big or relatively small. The black holes that used to be (**24**) _____ are quite common and are spotted when stars are close enough to have matter sucked into the black holes. Otherwise, the (**25**) _____ nature of black holes make them impossible to detect. There are also supermassive black holes that are theorised to be in the centre of nearly (**26**) _____. These are spotted by what happens around them.

READING PASSAGE 3

*You should spend about 20 minutes on **Questions 27 - 40**, which are based on Reading Passage 3 below.*

CCTV Surveillance

In recent years, a combination of perceptions and fears regarding increased street crime and advances in technology has seen an upsurge in the use of closed circuit television (CCTV) as a tool for tackling crime in public places. Many private companies and a number of local government authorities have initiated trials in the use of CCTV, and the technology is also being used in a number of ways in the public transport system.

Because CCTV is relatively new, it is still not clear how effective it is in deterring or reducing crime. Research evidence so far suggests that it is an effective strategy in situational crime prevention at a local level, but only as one of a range of crime prevention strategies. In addition, it appears from the research that CCTV is effective in addressing property crime and some types of assault and robbery. Of course, high-risk areas, for example jewellery shops, can greatly benefit from the visible deterrent of CCTV cameras.

Evidence also suggests that the benefits of CCTV surveillance fade after a period of time, and that displacement may occur, that is that the crime may simply move to other areas away from the CCTV surveillance, or there may be a shift to different sorts of crime that are less susceptible to CCTV surveillance. One important thing is that the reduction in crime that people believe CCTV brings can lead to enhanced perceptions of safety in a particular area, which makes communities happier and more satisfied with government actions.

In general, the issue of whether or not to consider implementing a CCTV scheme is likely to arise in response to a perception or awareness that there is a crime problem in a specific public place. This may be indicated by media coverage, by complaints to the council or other authorities or through police contact with the council. Once a local council identifies that there is a problem, it needs to form a Community Safety Committee, which should study a broad range of crime prevention and community safety issues and evaluate various options for dealing with them.

Installing and trialling a CCTV scheme usually involves decisions about technical, financial and operational matters that may be beyond the expertise of a Community Safety Committee. Therefore, the establishment of a specialised CCTV Committee may be the appropriate way of ensuring sound management of the scheme. Alternatively, a program co-ordinator with experience in developing community safety initiatives could be appointed to manage the development of the CCTV program. Both of these should offer expert advice to the Community Safety Committee.

The Community Safety Committee must carry out a crime assessment of the area where problems have been identified. The analysis should be conducted in consultation with local police, and, as appropriate, representatives of the local community. Once the crime assessment provides a clear picture of the nature of the criminal activities, a Crime Prevention Plan should be made. If the Committee believes that one of the strategies to address the problems identified in the crime assessment is the establishment of a CCTV program, it is essential that the Crime Prevention Plan outlines how this strategy is integrated with the broad plan objectives and why CCTV is considered appropriate.

There are various disadvantages and criticisms of CCTV. First is the perception that CCTV is an invasion of everyone's privacy. It is argued that the steady expansion in the surveillance apparatus of the state and private sector has diminished the privacy of every individual, has lessened people's trust in the state and poses a significant threat to personal privacy and individual freedom. Although in most countries there is nothing inherently unconstitutional in the use of surveillance by the state, there is nonetheless a danger that it may disturb some of the presumptions and relationships that underpin the relationship between the individual and the state. This is because mass surveillance promotes the view that everybody is untrustworthy. If governments gather data on people all the time, on the basis that they may do something wrong, this promotes a view that the citizens cannot be trusted.

There are also worries about the social effects of surveillance and the potential for discrimination. Cameras are installed so as to watch places and identified groups of people. Studies have shown that existing surveillance systems and databases with collected information may reflect institutional biases, often based on factors such as race.

Another problem with CCTV is the cost of installation and maintenance. As an example, over the last 20 years in the UK, approximately 78 per cent of the Home Office crime prevention budget was spent on installing CCTV. Where previously this money might have been spent on street lighting and supporting neighbourhood crime prevention initiatives, it is now used to maintain and expand the network of police and local authority cameras.

Protecting the public is a duty of government. However, surveillance and the use of collected personal information may lead to a conflict between the interests of the citizen and the goals of the state, and it has the potential to undermine privacy and limit the freedom of the individual. It seems that CCTV does not significantly stop crime, although when a crime has occurred, CCTV is a vital element of the investigative process. Therefore, as CCTV on its own can do little to address long-term crime prevention, CCTV should only be considered as one part of an integrated crime prevention strategy and should be installed on a trial basis subject to rigorous evaluation as to its usefulness.

Questions 27 – 29

Choose **THREE** letters, **A - F**.

According to the text, what **THREE** facts are advantages of using CCTV?

Write the correct letter, **A - F**, in any order in boxes **27 - 29** on your answer sheet.

A   CCTV can prevent property crime.

B   CCTV is a cheap way of monitoring the streets.

C   CCTV can be a preventative measure in specific locations identified as being threatened by crime.

D   CCTV is simple to install.

E   CCTV is particularly useful at military installations.

F   CCTV makes the community feel safer.

Questions 30 – 35

Complete the flow chart below.

*Write **NO MORE THAN THREE WORDS** from the text for each answer.*

*Write your answers in boxes **30 – 35** on your answer sheet.*

Setting up CCTV

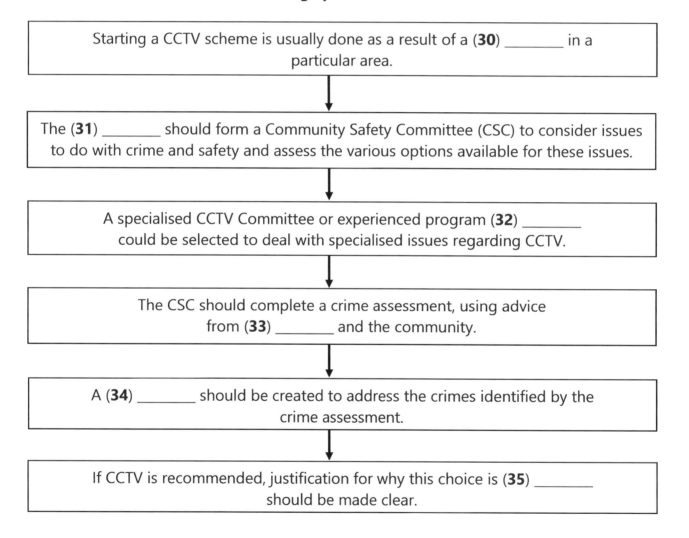

Starting a CCTV scheme is usually done as a result of a (**30**) _____ in a particular area.

↓

The (**31**) _____ should form a Community Safety Committee (CSC) to consider issues to do with crime and safety and assess the various options available for these issues.

↓

A specialised CCTV Committee or experienced program (**32**) _____ could be selected to deal with specialised issues regarding CCTV.

↓

The CSC should complete a crime assessment, using advice from (**33**) _____ and the community.

↓

A (**34**) _____ should be created to address the crimes identified by the crime assessment.

↓

If CCTV is recommended, justification for why this choice is (**35**) _____ should be made clear.

Questions 36 – 40

Complete the notes below.

Write **NO MORE THAN TWO WORDS** for each answer.

Write your answers in boxes **36 - 40** on your answer sheet.

---

* CCTV is seen as an invasion of privacy, as it is part of governments' (**36**) _____ ; it can lead to a loss of government trust in the public.

* Usually CCTV is not often (**37**) _____ , but it damages the government – public relationship due to its assumptions that the public are untrustworthy.

* Camera positioning has led to accusations of (**38**) _____ , as the locations can reveal (**39**) _____ .

* The installation and maintenance costs are high and take money away from other crime prevention initiatives.

* Surveillance in the name of protection has mixed benefits and drawbacks. It seems therefore that it should be used as part of an overall strategy with strict trials and (**40**) _____ to check its effectiveness.

WRITING

WRITING TASK 1

You should spend about 20 minutes on this task.

The bar chart below shows the US' top ten processed food export markets for last year and six years ago.

Summarise the information by selecting and reporting the main features, and make comparisons where relevant.

You should write at least 150 words.

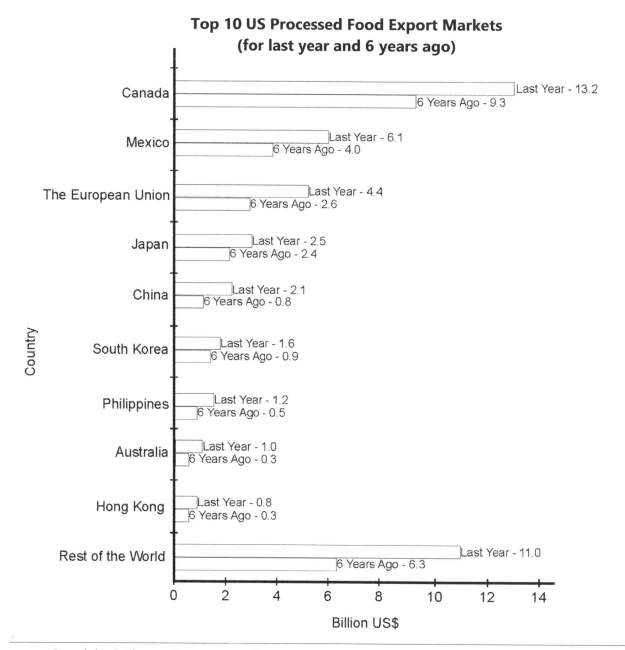

**Top 10 US Processed Food Export Markets
(for last year and 6 years ago)**

Canada — Last Year - 13.2 / 6 Years Ago - 9.3
Mexico — Last Year - 6.1 / 6 Years Ago - 4.0
The European Union — Last Year - 4.4 / 6 Years Ago - 2.6
Japan — Last Year - 2.5 / 6 Years Ago - 2.4
China — Last Year - 2.1 / 6 Years Ago - 0.8
South Korea — Last Year - 1.6 / 6 Years Ago - 0.9
Philippines — Last Year - 1.2 / 6 Years Ago - 0.5
Australia — Last Year - 1.0 / 6 Years Ago - 0.3
Hong Kong — Last Year - 0.8 / 6 Years Ago - 0.3
Rest of the World — Last Year - 11.0 / 6 Years Ago - 6.3

Country (y-axis)
Billion US$ (x-axis: 0, 2, 4, 6, 8, 10, 12, 14)

WRITING TASK 2

You should spend about 40 minutes on this task.

Write about the following topic:

In some countries, private cars are now banned from certain city centres.

What are the advantages of such a system and do you feel that this is something that most cities should adopt?

Give reasons for your answer and include any relevant examples from your knowledge or experience.

You should write at least 250 words.

SPEAKING

SECTION 1

- Can you tell me a little about your job or studies?
- Do you like the job or studies that you do at the moment? (Why/Why not?)
- Do you prefer to work or study in the morning or later in the day? (Why?)

Topic 1   Happiness
- What makes you happy?
- Does money make people happy?
- Do you think young people are the happiest people? (Why/Why not?)
- Why can pets make people happy?

Topic 2   Photography
- Do you like to take photographs? (Why/Why not?)
- Why do you think people like to keep photographs?
- Can taking photographs be an invasion of people's privacy? (Why?)
- What are the dangers of having photographs taken today with regards to the Internet?

SECTION 2

Describe a memorable teacher.
You should say:
        who this teacher was
        what this teacher taught
        where you knew this teacher
and briefly explain why this teacher is so memorable.

SECTION 3

Topic 1   Teachers
- What are the qualities that make a good teacher?
- Do you think that teachers are underpaid for what they do?
- What are the main challenges facing teachers today?
- What can governments do to improve the job that teachers have to do?

Topic 2   Education and Schools
- How do you think education has changed over the last 50 years?
- What role do parents have in their children's education?
- Do you think that private education is something that should be allowed in today's society? (Why/Why not?)
- Should education be delivered to single- or mixed-sex classes? (Why/Why not?)

Page 96

PRACTICE TEST 15

LISTENING

 Download audio recordings for the test here:
http://www.ielts-blog.com/ielts-practice-tests-downloads/

SECTION 1   *Questions 1 – 10*

Questions 1 – 6

Complete the hospital's new employee record sheet below.

*Write **NO MORE THAN THREE WORDS AND/OR A NUMBER** from the listening for each answer.*

<table>
<tr><td colspan="2" align="center">**New Employee Record Sheet**</td></tr>
<tr><td>***Example***</td><td>***Answer***</td></tr>
<tr><td>Job applied for:</td><td>***Cleaner***</td></tr>
<tr><td>Applicant's Name:</td><td>Adam (**1**) _____</td></tr>
<tr><td>Address:

Postcode:</td><td>82 Ackland Road
Gorley
OG8 6RE</td></tr>
<tr><td>Mobile Telephone:</td><td>07543 842 (**2**) _____</td></tr>
<tr><td>National Insurance Number:</td><td>MA 67 95 36 F</td></tr>
<tr><td>Age:</td><td>(**3**) _____</td></tr>
<tr><td>Times Available:</td><td>6 a.m. - 9 a.m. & after 3 p.m. - 10 p.m.
(**4**) _____ at weekends</td></tr>
<tr><td>Experience:</td><td>Weekend job at a (**5**) _____ - washed up, cleaned surfaces and floors
David at david@apple.com can provide us with a (**6**) _____</td></tr>
</table>

Questions 7 – 10

Complete Adam's notes below.

Use **NO MORE THAN TWO WORDS** from the listening for each answer.

When I arrive and leave, I need to sign in and out at the (**7**) _____ - this ensures my work times and pay are correct. I get £9 an hour.

In the staff changing rooms, I must change into overalls and a (**8**) _____.

Every 3 hours I get a break - I can go outside or go to the (**9**) _____, where I can get a drink; if I work longer than 4 hours, I get a meal.

I will start next Saturday at 9 a.m.

I need to come in as well for (**10**) _____ on Thursday at 4 p.m. (I'll be paid for this).

SECTION 2   *Questions 11 - 20*

Questions 11 – 16

Complete the summary below on the radio talk on the town exhibition.

*Write **NO MORE THAN TWO WORDS** from the listening for each answer.*

The Town Exhibition

The town exhibition will be found in the (**11**) _____ from the 9th July to the
14th July. The exhibition firstly is a show for local businesses, especially for apple
products. Secondly, the exhibition is a town fair, with lots of games and
amusements. The latter mainly starts from (**12**) _____ p.m. The exhibition ends
nightly with a fireworks display at 10 p.m., which is at the central lake. This final
show can often upset (**13**) _____, so it's best to leave them behind. There will be
plenty of international food and drinks on offer and an open fire barbecue
offering freshly grilled meats and (**14**) _____.

Please dress children suitably and don't forget sun cream and a hat if it's sunny. In
bad weather, don't forget raincoats and umbrellas; consider wearing (**15**) _____,
which will help if it's very muddy.

There will be a lottery every evening, with results given just before the fireworks.
Tickets are a dollar for 4. Write your name and (**16**) _____ on the back of your
tickets if you can't stay for the results.

Questions 17 – 20

*Below is a plan of the town exhibition with **6** locations marked **A** - **F**.*

*Questions **17** - **20** name **4** places that can be visited at the exhibition.*

*Write the correct letter (**A** - **F**) that matches the places that can be visited with their locations.*

17	Exhibition on other local businesses	_____
18	The first aid station	_____
19	Food stations	_____
20	Amusement rides	_____

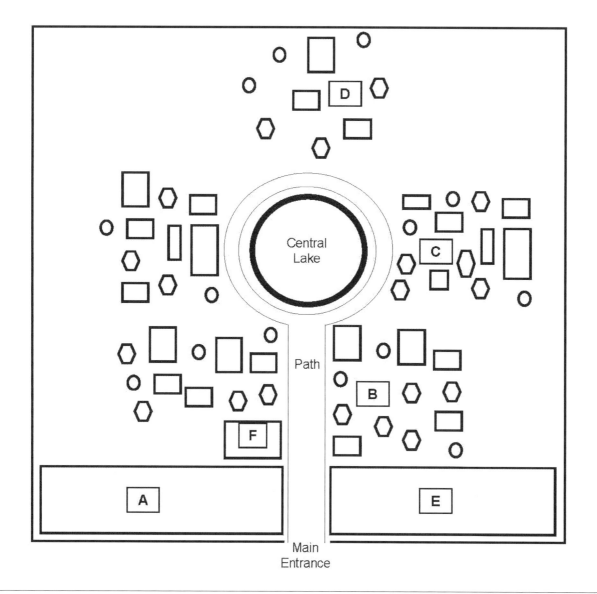

SECTION 3   *Questions 21 – 30*

Questions 21 – 25

*Choose the correct letter **A, B, or C**.*

21   Two years ago, the US had to import approximately

    A   a third of its petroleum needs.
    B   half of its petroleum needs.
    C   three quarters of its petroleum needs.

22   Generating electricity on board a car is not usually done, because

    A   onboard generators are too heavy.
    B   onboard generators are too bulky.
    C   it's not an economic way of powering a car.

23   Electric cars have cheaper fuel costs mainly because

    A   conventional fuel is more expensive than electricity.
    B   electric cars are lighter than conventional cars.
    C   electric cars are slower than conventional cars.

24   Electric cars' lifecycle emissions depend on

    A   the type of electric motor used in the cars.
    B   where in the US the electricity used for power is generated.
    C   the speed at which the cars are driven.

25   Biofuel B100's emissions are compensated for by

    A   the lack of carbon dioxide that is generated by the biodiesel engine.
    B   the number people who have switched to using the fuel.
    C   the growth of the source plants for the fuel.

Questions 26 – 30

Complete the table below.

Write **NO MORE THAN TWO WORDS** from the listening for each answer.

The Disadvantages of Electric Cars	
Refuelling Infrastructure	* Not as common as gas stations * Relevant organisations are expanding the network * Potentially available anywhere people park * Hybrids can use a (**26**) _____ when necessary
Purchase Costs	* Much higher than conventional cars * Prices will drop as (**27**) _____ grow * Purchase costs can be offset by fuel savings, tax credits and state (**28**) _____
Maintenance	* Similar to conventional cars, except the battery * Batteries will wear out in spite of their design for extended life * Some manufacturers offer different types of (**29**) _____ for batteries * Battery life a big disadvantage - can be expensive to replace * Improvements in (**30**) _____ and greater manufacturing output will lead to lower battery prices

SECTION 4   *Questions 31 – 40*

Questions 31 – 40

*Complete the notes below. Use **NO MORE THAN THREE WORDS** from the listening for each answer.*

Twin Languages

Twin languages are officially called autonomous languages; not a (**31**) _____ event - occurs in approx. 40% of twins.

Formulation

Because twins are so close, they don't communicate so much with others and they develop their own communication system.
It's not always between twins - it's evident also in close siblings.
It usually occurs with the lack of an (**32**) _____ .
Autonomous languages usually consist of onomatopoeic utterances, some (**33**) _____ and normal language adapted by children within their speech limitations.
Autonomous languages lack morphology and have a strange word order.
Autonomous languages are hard for other people to understand.

Research

Only (**34**) _____ can explain how and why autonomous languages emerge.
Autonomous languages could arise in children with phonology delays due to little or no language sources to copy.
Children normally develop speech in the same way and make the same (**35**) _____ when talking.
Phonological delays can produce similar language to a "twin language".
Autonomous languages can be (**36**) _____ in twins and close siblings as they communicate in a similar way.
(**37**) _____ is often needed to help with sound development.
Autonomous languages have also been linked to language delays at school.

Parents

Parents needn't worry too much - children can switch between secret and normal languages.
Not all children using an autonomous language will have language delays.
An autonomous language is a (**38**) _____ for speech and language problems - a therapist would probably be helpful.
Parents are the best guide for children's language - they influence sound development and the children's length of (**39**) _____ .
Parents should therefore talk as much as possible to their children.
(**40**) _____ is very beneficial for all children, especially twins.

Conclusion

Autonomous languages usually disappear after intervention or interaction with other children at school.
Children might occasionally revert to the autonomous language (normal), but with care, this will not lead to language problems.

READING

READING PASSAGE 1

*You should spend about 20 minutes on **Questions 1 - 13**, which are based on Reading Passage 1 below.*

The Lake Erie Canal

Begun in 1817 and opened in its entirety in 1825, the Erie Canal is considered by some to be the engineering marvel of the nineteenth century. When the federal government concluded that the project was too ambitious to undertake, the State of New York took on the task of carving 363 miles of canal through the wilderness, with nothing but the muscle power of men and horses.

Once derided as 'Clinton's Folly' for the Governor who lent his vision and political muscle to the project, the Erie Canal experienced unparalleled success almost overnight. The iconic waterway established settlement patterns for most of the United States during the nineteenth century, made New York the financial capital of the world, provided a critical supply line that helped the North win the Civil War, and precipitated a series of social and economic changes throughout a young America.

Explorers had long searched for a water route to the west. Throughout the eighteenth and nineteenth centuries, the lack of an efficient and safe transportation network kept populations and trade largely confined to coastal areas. At the beginning of the nineteenth century, the Allegheny Mountains were the Western Frontier. The Northwest Territories that would later become Illinois, Indiana, Michigan and Ohio were rich in timber, minerals, and fertile land for farming, but it took weeks to reach these things. Travellers were faced with rutted turnpike roads that baked to hardness in the summer sun. In the winter, the roads dissolved into mud.

An imprisoned flour merchant named Jesse Hawley envisioned a better way: a canal from Buffalo on the eastern shore of Lake Erie to Albany on the upper Hudson River, a distance of almost 400 miles. Long a proponent of efficient water transportation, Hawley had gone bankrupt trying to move his products to market. Hawley's ideas caught the interest of Assemblyman Joshua Forman, who submitted the first state legislation related to the Erie Canal in 1808, calling for a series of surveys to be made examining the practicality of a water route between Lake Erie and the Hudson River. In 1810, Thomas Eddy, and State Senator Jonas Platt, hoping to get plans for the canal moving forward, approached influential Senator De Witt Clinton, former mayor of New York City, to enlist his support. Though Clinton had been recruited to the canal effort by Eddy and Platt, he quickly became one of the canal's most active supporters and went on to successfully tie his very political fate to its success. On April 15th, 1817, the New York State Legislature finally approved construction of the Erie Canal. The Legislature authorised $7 million for construction of the 363-mile long waterway, which was to be 40 feet wide and eighteen feet deep. Construction began on July 4th 1817 and took eight years.

Like most canals, the Erie Canal depended on a lock system in order to compensate for changes in water levels over distance. A lock is a section of canal or river that is closed off to control the water level, so that boats can be raised or lowered as they pass through it. Locks have two sets of sluice gates (top and bottom), which seal off and then open the entrances to the chamber, which is where a boat waits while the movement up or down takes place. In addition, locks also have valves at the bottom of the sluice gates and it is by opening these valves that water is allowed into and out of the chamber to raise or lower the water level, and hence the boat.

The effect of the Erie Canal was both immediate and dramatic, and settlers poured west. The explosion of trade prophesied by Governor Clinton began, spurred by freight rates from Buffalo to New York of $10 per ton by canal, compared with $100 per ton by road. In 1829, there were 3,640 bushels of wheat transported down the canal from Buffalo. By 1837, this figure had increased to 500,000 bushels and, four years later, it reached one million. In nine years, canal tolls more than recouped the entire cost of construction. Within 15 years of the canal's opening, New York was the busiest port in America, moving tonnages greater than Boston, Baltimore and New Orleans combined. Today, it can still be seen that every major city in New York State falls along the trade route established by the Erie Canal and nearly 80 per cent of upstate New York's inhabitants live within 25 miles of the Erie Canal.

The completion of the Erie Canal spurred the first great westward movement of American settlers, gave access to the resources west of the Appalachians and made New York the preeminent commercial city in the United States. At one time, more than 50,000 people depended on the Erie Canal for their livelihood. From its inception, the Erie Canal helped form a whole new culture revolving around canal life. For those who travelled along the canal in packet boats or passenger vessels, the canal was an exciting place. Gambling and entertainment were frequent pastimes, and often families would meet each year at the same locations to share stories and adventures. Today, the canal has returned to its former glory and is filled with pleasure boats, fishermen, holidaymakers and cyclists riding the former towpaths where mules once trod. The excitement of the past is alive and well.

Questions 1 – 6

*Choose **SIX** letters, **A** - **K**.*

*What **SIX** of the following were effects of the Lake Erie Canal?*

*Write the correct letter, **A** - **K**, in any order in boxes **1** - **6** on your answer sheet.*

A   It brought building materials to expand the city of Chicago.

B   It established the financial dominance of New York City.

C   It generated taxes that stimulated the whole region.

D   It helped the north win the US Civil War.

E   It was used for training troops in World War One.

F   It helped boost a politician's career.

G   It stimulated the shipbuilding industry.

H   It led to cheaper distribution for goods.

I   It influenced New York State's population distribution.

J   It allowed damaging species of fish to travel to different ecosystems.

K   It became a boost for tourism.

Questions 7 – 9

Label the diagram below.

Write **NO MORE THAN TWO WORDS** from the text for each answer.

Write your answers in boxes **7 - 9** on your answer sheet.

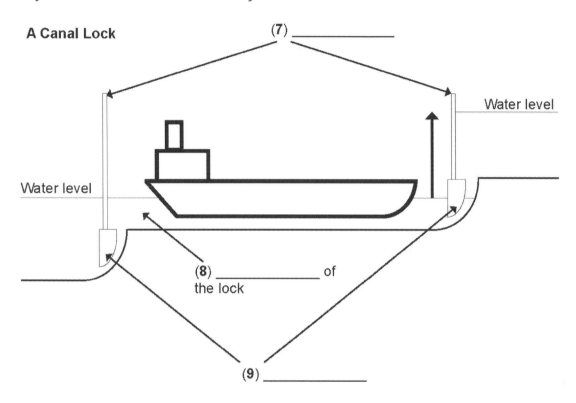

Questions 10 – 13

Answer the questions below.

Write **NO MORE THAN TWO WORDS AND/OR A NUMBER** from the text for each answer.

Write your answers in boxes **10 - 13** on your answer sheet.

10   What was the beneficial factor for productive agriculture in the Northwest Territories at the beginning of the nineteenth century?

11   In what commodity did the person who first came up with the idea of the Erie Canal trade?

12   How long did it take to build the Erie Canal?

13   How were the Erie Canal's building costs recovered?

READING PASSAGE 2

*You should spend about 20 minutes on **Questions 14 - 26**, which are based on Reading Passage 2 below.*

The Story of Opium

Paragraph A
Opium is a substance that is derived by collecting and later drying the milky juice that comes from the seed pods of the poppy plant. The substance can vary in colour and may be yellow or could range all the way to a very dark brown colour. Opium has a very bitter taste that is comparable to other plants from similar families and a distinct odour that is clearly identifiable. The primary component of opium is twelve per cent morphine, which is an alkaloid that is often processed chemically to produce illegal drugs, such as heroin. Codeine and other non-narcotic alkaloids are also found in the latex that is derived from the opium poppy plant.

Paragraph B
The history of opium dates back as far as the Neolithic and ancient times, when the drug was widely used in anaesthesia, as well as for ritualistic purposes. In ancient Egypt, opium was used as an analgesic and the Indians as well as the Romans both used opium during surgical procedures. Throughout the American Civil War, opium and various derivatives of opium were used. Morphine, opiods and synthetic opiates are all derived or come directly from the opium poppy, even in today's medical use. While the medical world has evolved greatly and has manipulated opium to meet the needs of patients, the most raw form of opium, morphine, continues to be one of the most widely used analgesic drugs, even today.

Paragraph C
Opium use has many long- and short-term consequences that can be harmful to the body. Initially, the euphoric state that is caused by the drug can be relaxing and comforting, but long-term use of opium can lead to addiction and physical dependence. Many of the harmful consequences of using opium are related to the damage caused to the lungs from smoking the drug or to the consequences that are caused by derivatives of the drug. For many, the harmful consequences of opium will not present themselves until many years of use. However, for some, the effects of opium use are dangerous almost immediately and an overdose can lead to a risk of death.

Paragraph D
Today, heroin's long journey to final use begins with the planting of opium poppy seeds. Opium is grown mainly by impoverished farmers on small plots in remote regions of the world. It flourishes in dry, warm climates and the vast majority of opium poppies are grown in a narrow, 4,500-mile stretch of mountains extending across central Asia from Turkey through Pakistan and Burma. Recently, opium has been grown in Latin America, notably Colombia and Mexico. The farmer takes his crop of opium to the nearest village, where he will sell it to the dealer who offers him the best price.

Paragraph E
Legal growing of opium for medicinal use currently takes place in India, Turkey, and Australia. Two thousand tons of opium are produced annually and this supplies the world with the raw material needed to make medicinal products. Traditionally, opium was obtained from the latex of the poppy plant by scoring the seed pods by hand and allowing the latex to leak out and dry up. The sticky yellowish/brown residue is then scraped off and harvested for use. Today, modern methods of opium harvest include processing the mature poppy plant by machine in order to get the latex out of the flowering plant. Overall, opium production has changed very little over the years, however, selective breeding of the plant has led to an increase in the content of the phenanthrene alkaloids morphine, codeine and thebaine. Currently, there are three main sources for illegal opium: Burma, Afghanistan, and Colombia. Opium and heroin are ideal trade products: they are in great demand, are very profitable to produce, and the products take up little space. With modern transportation, opium and heroin can be moved from one country to another within days or a few weeks. Both drugs have a long and stable shelf life, allowing the products to be stored for long periods of time.

Paragraph F
Opium was used for recreational purposes in China during the fifteenth century and on through the seventeenth century. It was nearly 300 years before the Chinese first realised that smoking opium was actually dangerous and could lead to physical dependence. In 1909, the International Opium Commission was formed to help regulate the shipping, sale and use of opium due to the dangers that were now widely known pertaining to the regular use of the drug. At this time, opium was first being purified into morphine and heroin, which are both highly potent drugs that have proved to be very much more dangerous than the raw opium itself. Recreational use of these drugs is now illegal in most countries around the world.

Paragraph G
In the early days, people did not worry too much about the physical dependence that opium and its derivatives created. Today, the dangers are well recognised and there are a variety of ways to help people who have fallen victim to it. Most of the time, inpatient or residential treatment will be the basis for recovery. These programs will utilise counselling in both individual and group sessions to provide a foundation for success in recovery. Following the counselling in an inpatient treatment facility, those in recovery will continue treatment in an outpatient facility that provides similar counselling and therapy in a less supervised environment.

Questions 14 – 20

*The text on the previous pages has 7 paragraphs (**A – G**).*

Choose the correct heading for each paragraph from the list of headings below.

*Write the correct number (**i – x**) in boxes **14 – 20** on your answer sheet.*

i	From Seed to Sale
ii	Government Agencies Chase Criminals
iii	Illegal Use
iv	Origins
v	Modern Production
vi	Effects
vii	High Profits Cause Conflicts
viii	Treating Addiction
ix	What is it?
x	Famous Users

14   Paragraph A

15   Paragraph B

16   Paragraph C

17   Paragraph D

18   Paragraph E

19   Paragraph F

20   Paragraph G

Questions 21 – 23

*Choose the correct letter **A, B, C or D**.*

*Write the correct letter in boxes **21 - 23** on your answer sheet.*

21   Opium can be easily recognised by

     A   its smell.
     B   its colour.
     C   its taste.
     D   its packaging.

22   Opium has been used throughout history as

     A   a drug to induce childbirth.
     B   a poison.
     C   a pain reliever.
     D   a currency.

23   The dangerous properties of opium are

     A   always apparent quite a long time after the first use.
     B   not often experienced by users.
     C   never experienced if opium is used in moderation.
     D   sometimes experienced straight away in some users.

Questions 24 – 26

Complete the sentences below.

*Write **NO MORE THAN TWO WORDS** from the text for each answer.*

*Write your answers in boxes **24 - 26** on your answer sheet.*

24   The medicinal content of opium has been increased by the _____ of the opium poppy.

25   It was the _____ who first found that using opium was harmful.

26   _____ for groups and individuals is often used to treat people addicted to opium.

READING PASSAGE 3

*You should spend about 20 minutes on **Questions 27 - 40**, which are based on Reading Passage 3 below*

Video Games and Violence

For quite some time now, video games that involve significant amounts of violence have been blamed for growing numbers of violence by young people, the demographic most likely to play these games. Debate about this has even reached the courts, with both sides of the argument claiming that the scientific literature supports their opinions. Some experts involved have proclaimed that the debate is scientifically settled and that only people holding personal concerns and biases oppose these established truths. Scientifically, two competing social theories have been formulated about the potential effects of video game violence. The first is that video games increase violence because they teach players how to be violent and reinforce violent tendencies. The second theory is that video games have a possibly beneficial effect, because they provide a socially acceptable outlet for the release of aggression and thereby promote better mental health.

Articles reviewing the effects of video games on general populations have found links between playing violent video games and changes in behaviour, and/or thought process, with some finding that people who played realistic violent games for 45 minutes had a greater increase in violent and aggressive feelings than persons who played unrealistic violent video games or non-violent video games for the same period. What seems clear though is that certain populations are more at risk and/or are more likely to play violent video games than others. Studies suggest that at-risk individuals are usually male, have pre-existing personality disorders or traits, for example a conduct disorder, have pre-existing mental health conditions, have had difficult or traumatic upbringings, and are insecure with poor self-esteem. Children with attention deficit disorder were also seen to be at a higher risk of showing addictive behaviour to violent video games and that violent video games might be a significant risk variable for aggressive behaviour in persons who already have aggressive personality traits. There are, of course, plenty of other groups of people (probably the majority of users) who play and enjoy video games, with or without violence, that have no character disorders at all. Another recent key report which relied on parents' self-report of their children's video game–playing behaviours suggests that spending a large amount of time playing violent video games was correlated with troublesome behaviour and poor academic achievement. The same study also indicated that children who played more educational games had more positive outcomes.

What is interesting is that the comic book debate of the 1950's is eerily similar when compared to the current debate about the effects of video games on children. In 1954, the US Senate Subcommittee on Juvenile Delinquency held hearings on the effects of comic books on America's youth. The primary focus of the Senate hearings was 'crime and horror' comic books, some of which graphically showed horrific images, such as dismembered bodies. Concerns were voiced that these comics would lead to a decline in public morals, an increase in violence and aggression, an increase in general lawlessness, and societal disrespect and deterioration. Medical and social science experts became involved in the debate, writing articles in reputable journals. Many of the concerns that dominate the current video game debate were also expressed and it could show the frequently experienced perception that violent behaviour is always more prevalent in the present than in the past and that people just search for a scapegoat on which to blame it.

Although many articles have suggested a connection between violent video games and aggression, several studies have found no such relationship. One study in fact showed that non-gamers and excessive gamers both had lower self-reported mental wellness scores than low to moderate gamers. This finding suggests that excessive playing may be detrimental, but that there are some protective and non-harmful consequences to playing in moderation. This finding is in line with social theory, which suggests that video games, like sports, may provide an outlet for individuals to work through aggression and, therefore, have better mental functioning and overall lower levels of aggression. The same study pointed to the positive attributes of violent video game playing, such as improved visual-spatial coordination, increased peripheral attention, and increased decision-making capabilities. People who play a lot of video games also generally have better overall computer skills than people who do not.

Another study examining the multivariate risk issues for youth violence showed that the most common positive predictors of youth violence were delinquent peer influences, antisocial personality traits, depression, and parents or guardians who use psychological abuse in family relationships. The factors that were not found to be predictive of youth violence included neighbourhood quality, parental use of domestic physical violence in intimate relationships, and exposure to violent television or video games.

A recent neurological study provided further evidence that video games do not increase violent behaviour by users. The study examined whether there was a change in brain imaging that suggested a loss of distinction between virtual and actual violence in players of violent video games compared with controls. What was found was that the ability to differentiate automatically between real and virtual violence was not diminished by a long-term history of violent video game play, and nor were gamers' neural responses to real violence subject to desensitisation processes. This would indicate that video games do not cause people to lose their grip on what is real in comparison with what is fantasy.

Many questions are raised by the split nature of the scientific literature regarding violence and video games and it should also be remembered that a correlation does not prove a causation. Stakeholders need to examine the current video game debate in order to decide how to sensibly influence social policy.

Questions 27 – 33

Do the following statements agree with the information given in the text?

In boxes **27 – 33** on your answer sheet write:

TRUE	if the statement agrees with the information
FALSE	if the statement contradicts the information
NOT GIVEN	if there is no information on this

27   Violent video games are most likely to be played by people in their youth and middle age.

28   It has been claimed that people who still feel the effects of violent video games are not decided and clear have vested interests in the debate.

29   It is claimed that men and women are more or less equally threatened by the effects of violent video games.

30   One study has found a link between usage of violent video games and poor school performance.

31   Various violent video games are based on stories previously published in comic books.

32   Some of the comic books of the 1950's had shocking images of mutilated people.

33   It has been claimed that violence has always been present in society and video games are just the latest thing to blame it on.

Questions 34 – 39

Complete the table below.

*Write **NO MORE THAN THREE WORDS** from the text for each answer.*

*Write your answers in boxes **34 - 39** on your answer sheet.*

Studies Defending the Use of Violent Video Games	
Study 1	* Non-gamers and excessive gamers had similar grading in terms of **(34)** _____. * It shows excessive gaming can have protective effects. * Similar ideas in social theory – users can rid themselves of **(35)** _____ and therefore have a better mental condition. * Gaming can improve visual-spatial coordination, peripheral attention, **(36)** _____ and computer skills.
Study 2	* It examined the various risk factors for youth violence – peers, personality, depression and psychological abuse. * Non-factors were **(37)** _____, violence at home and violent TV and video games.
Study 3	* A neurological study examining variations in **(38)** _____ when users interacted with virtual or real violence. * Results showed that users' differentiation between virtual or real violence was not affected by the use of violent video games. * The **(39)** _____ with regards to real violence in users' neural reactions were also not affected. * It shows video games do not affect people's perceptions of what is real or what is fantasy.

Question 40

*Choose the correct letter, **A, B, C or D**.*

*Write the correct letter in box **40** on your answer sheet.*

40   What is the writer's purpose in Reading Passage 3?

    A   To defend the use of violent video game usage.

    B   To discourage people from using violent video games.

    C   To examine examples of violence by users of violent video games.

    D   To review what has been discovered about the effects of violent video games.

WRITING

WRITING TASK 1

You should spend about 20 minutes on this task.

The flow charts below show the vicious circles of poverty at the institutional and individual levels.

Summarise the information by selecting and reporting the main features, and make comparisons where relevant.

You should write at least 150 words.

The Vicious Circle of Poverty - at the institutional level

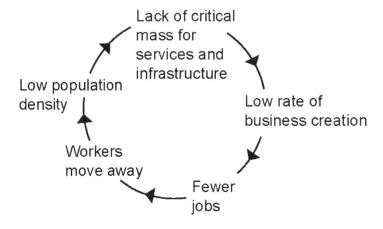

The Vicious Circle of Poverty - at the individual level

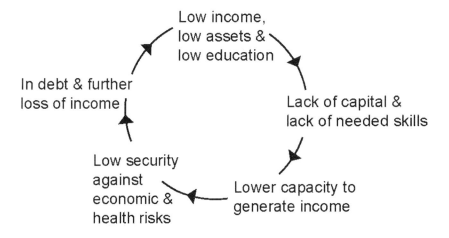

WRITING TASK 2

You should spend about 40 minutes on this task.

Write about the following topic:

There are many things that can motivate people to perform well in their work. These can include the salary, job satisfaction or the chance to help others.

What do you feel is the best motivation to do well at work?

Give reasons for your answer and include any relevant examples from your knowledge or experience.

You should write at least 250 words.

SPEAKING

SECTION 1

- Where do you work/study?
- How do you travel to work/study?
- What is the best thing about your job/studies?

Topic 1   Football
- Do you like football? (Why/Why not?)
- Why do you think football is so popular around the world?
- Why do you think so many people support their country or a particular team?
- Why do you think so much violence happens amongst people who watch football?

Topic 2   Being in Another Country
- What is the most interesting foreign country that you have visited? (Why?)
- What kind of things do you do when you visit a different country?
- What are some of things that are surprising when you have gone to a different country?
- What are some of the problems that happen when two people from different countries marry?

SECTION 2

> Describe your first mobile/cell phone.
> You should say:
>   when you got this mobile/cell phone
>   how much it cost
>   what it looked like
> and explain how different it is from the mobile/cell phone you use nowadays.

SECTION 3

Topic 1   Mobile/Cell Phones
- How have mobile phones changed life today?
- Do you think the use of mobile phones is overpriced?
- How do you think mobile phones will change over the next 50 years?
- Do you think young people spend too much time and money on their mobile phones? (Why?)

Topic 2   Technology
- What part of modern technology could you not do without today?
- Could you compare society's dependence on technology today with 50 years ago?
- What are some of the disadvantages of society's dependence on technology today?
- How will education systems have to change so that today's youth can use and improve today's technology?

Listening Test Answer Sheet

1		21	
2		22	
3		23	
4		24	
5		25	
6		26	
7		27	
8		28	
9		29	
10		30	
11		31	
12		32	
13		33	
14		34	
15		35	
16		36	
17		37	
18		38	
19		39	
20		40	

Reading Test Answer Sheet

1		21	
2		22	
3		23	
4		24	
5		25	
6		26	
7		27	
8		28	
9		29	
10		30	
11		31	
12		32	
13		33	
14		34	
15		35	
16		36	
17		37	
18		38	
19		39	
20		40	

Answers

LISTENING ANSWERS

/ indicates an alternative answer   ( ) indicates an optional answer

TEST 11	TEST 12	TEST 13	TEST 14	TEST 15
1. 6 months	1. B	1. Gloria	1. coaches	1. Marshall
2. email	2. B	2. 40	2. first aid	2. 592
3. photo(card)	3. C	3. 451	3. sports complex	3. 21
4. 5%	4. C	4. (Bank) transfer	4. fruit	4. mornings
5. signature	5. A	5. (To) cats	5. snacks	5. (local) restaurant
6. E	6. hills	6. 8.30	6. 4.30	6. reference
7. A	7. bus	7. (changes of) clothing	7. C	7. (staff) reception
8. D	8. 5	8. nurse	8. C	8. (special) hat
9. B	9. picnic	9. (information) pack	9. A	9. (staff) canteen
10. E	10. map	10. weekend(s)	10. A	10. (some) training
11. (The) (town) council	11. B*	11. 60	11. E	11. (town) park
12. Every 6 months	12. E*	12. (married) couples	12. D	12. 3
13. (The) interactive classroom	13. A°	13. (specialised) diets	13. B	13. dogs
14. 3 hours	14. D°	14. independent	14. A	14. vegetables
15. 2 p.m.	15. F°	15. website	15. H	15. (rubber) boots
16. self-assessment test	16. D	16. guest	16. Opportunity	16. (telephone) number
17. bookkeeping	17. B	17. brain	17. locations	17. A
18. Computers for Photography	18. C	18. 1-day	18. signal	18. F
19. shortcuts	19. H	19. isolation	19. (user) manual	19. D
20. skills	20. A	20. (special) tools	20. brand	20. C
21. Broadband	21. D	21. B	21. tourism	21. A
22. bias	22. A	22. A	22. budget	22. C
23. notice (periods)	23. H	23. C	23. (exchange) rates	23. A
24. tariff(s) (information)	24. B	24. B	24. (import) duty	24. B
25. profit	25. G	25. C	25. taxes	25. C
26. (signal) (reception)	26. sand	26. Well head	26. transportation	26. fossil fuel
27. C	27. high tide	27. Cap rock	27. quality	27. production (volumes)
28. A	28. undercut	28. (Underground) sensors	28. biodiversity	28. incentives
29. (statistical) analysis	29. (The) coastguard	29. (by) satellite	29. water	29. warranty
30. cinema	30. (Our) (mobile) phones	30. 4 weeks	30. pest control	30. technology
31. decay	31. (overall) personality	31. influence	31. intervals	31. rare
32. standard of living	32. mean (intelligence)	32. subconscious	32. moist soil	32. (adult) (model) language / (adult) model
33. 2	33. verbal	33. concentration	33. leaves	33. invented words
34. earthquakes	34. (psychological) test	34. relaxation	34. revenue	34. situational factors
35. (active) volcanic zones	35. literacy	35. sense organs	35. machine	35. errors
36. steam (vents)	36. extreme ends	36. potential	36. (monetary) loan	36. prolonged
37. transient	37. (the) interpretation	37. homework	37. protein	37. (Speech) therapy
38. (High pressure) steam / (Corrosive) steam	38. (brain) damage	38. C	38. (a) holding tank	38. (risk) factor
39. (A) (local) substation	39. school	39. E	39. slipstream	39. sentence
40. (A) cooling tower	40. reliability	40. G	40. coarse	40. Reading
	Note: *Answers for qu. 11 + 12, and for qu. 13, 14 + 15 can be written in any order			

READING ANSWERS

/ indicates an alternative answer   ( ) indicates an optional answer

TEST 11	TEST 12	TEST 13	TEST 14	TEST 15
1. A	1. FALSE	1. ix	1. D	1. B*
2. C	2. NOT GIVEN	2. iii	2. B	2. D*
3. D	3. FALSE	3. vi	3. G	3. F*
4. (The) amygdala	4. avalanche	4. i	4. C	4. H*
5. 10%	5. stability	5. viii	5. E	5. I*
6. (Their) personality	6. temperatures	6. x	6. A	6. K*
7. graded	7. warm air	7. iv	7. F	7. (Sluice) gates
8. therapist	8. dripping	8. A*	8. (index) fingers	8. (The) chamber
9. (negative) thoughts	9. elevated	9. C*	9. soldiers	9. Valves
10. behaviour	10. (air) vent	10. E*	10. (phonetic) sound	10. Fertile land
11. psychotherapy	11. (reindeer) hides	11. G*	11. awl	11. Flour
12. endorphins	12. melt	12. brick	12. contractions	12. 8 years
13. insomnia	13. (interior) decorations	13. (brightly) (coloured) uniforms	13. hardware	13. (Canal) tolls
14. C	14. spread	14. AH	14. FALSE	14. ix
15. D	15. reputations	15. AW	15. TRUE	15. iv
16. F	16. hide	16. GP	16. NOT GIVEN	16. vi
17. A	17. origins	17. JG	17. TRUE	17. i
18. D	18. risks	18. TM	18. (The) photon sphere	18. v
19. E	19. (Floppy) disks	19. AB	19. (The) singularity	19. iii
20. B	20. (A) logic bomb	20. SF	20. electrocardiogram	20. viii
21. C	21. (A) worm	21. 50	21. mass	21. A
22. B	22. Mutation	22. 2%	22. disk	22. C
23. A	23. Email	23. 50%	23. (cyclical) variations	23. D
24. FALSE	24. variants	24. A	24. massive stars	24. selective breeding
25. TRUE	25. (A) (regular) subscription	25. C	25. isolated	25. Chinese
26. NOT GIVEN	26. education of users	26. A	26. all large galaxies	26. Counselling
27. longevity	27. E	27. (unconscious) barriers	27. A*	27. FALSE
28. less developed countries	28. C	28. obsession	28. C*	28. TRUE
29. more developed nations	29. G	29. parent	29. F*	29. FALSE
30. reform	30. A	30. YES	30. crime problem	30. TRUE
31. contributions	31. D	31. NO	31. (local) council	31. NOT GIVEN
32. generations	32. F	32. NO	32. co-ordinator	32. TRUE
33. (historical) precedent	33. B	33. NOT GIVEN	33. (local) police	33. TRUE
34. NO	34. A	34. YES	34. Crime Prevention Plan	34. (mental) wellness scores
35. NO	35. C	35. Diminishing returns	35. appropriate	35. aggression
36. YES	36. C	36. factors	36. surveillance (apparatus)	36. decision-making (capabilities)
37. NOT GIVEN	37. B	37. career satisfaction	37. unconstitutional	37. neighbourhood (quality)
38. YES	38. YES	38. simple things	38. discrimination	38. brain imaging
39. NO	39. NO	39. (Cognitive) (dissonance) experiments	39. (institutional) biases	39. desensitisation (processes)
40. B	40. NOT GIVEN	40. (monetary) reward	40. (rigorous) evaluation	40. D
		Note: *Answers for qu. 8, 9, 10 + 11 in any order	**Note**: *Answers for qu. 31, 32 + 33 in any order	**Note**: *Answers for qu. 1, 2, 3, 4, 5 + 6 in any order

READING ANSWERS HELP

This section shows fragments of passages that contain the correct answers. If you have trouble locating the correct answer in the text, or can't understand why a particular answer is correct, refer to this section to understand the reasoning behind the answers. A group of answers with answers being preceded by * means that this group of answers may be given in any order. Answers in brackets () are optional answers.

ACADEMIC READING TEST 11

1. **A**   Anxiety is a common experience that can be a useful motivator or even lifesaver in situations that are objectively dangerous.

2. **C**   it can get problematic if the danger is one that is imagined rather than real, or the danger is something that is exaggerated.

3. **D**   About 17 per cent of the population will have an anxiety disorder at some stage in their life.

4. **(The) amygdala**   Using brain imaging technology and neurochemical techniques, scientists have discovered that the amygdala plays a significant role in most anxiety disorders.

5. **10%**   Only 10 per cent of people with an anxiety disorder will seek treatment.

6. **(Their) personality**   Most people tend to think they have had it for most of their lives, so it is just their personality and they cannot change their personality, and so they feel rather hopeless about it.

7. **graded**   The first psychotherapy treatment that was shown to be effective was exposure therapy, which essentially encourages people in a graded way to go into their feared situations and stay in them as long as they can and build up their confidence that way.

8. **therapist**   Often, the therapist will accompany the person to a feared situation to provide support and guidance.

9. **(negative) thoughts**   Group cognitive behaviour therapy has also been shown to be effective. This is a talking therapy that helps people to understand the link between negative thoughts and mood

10. **behaviour**   Group cognitive behaviour therapy has also been shown to be effective. This is a talking therapy that helps people to understand the link between negative thoughts and mood and how altering their behaviour can enable them to manage anxiety and feel in control.

11. **psychotherapy**   There are, of course, drugs that can help people with anxiety. Medication will not cure an anxiety disorder, but it can keep it under control while the person receives psychotherapy.

12. **endorphins**   There is plenty of evidence that exercise can help with anxiety problems. When stress affects the brain, with its many nerve connections, the rest of the body feels the impact as well. Exercise and other physical activity produce endorphins, which are chemicals in the brain that act as natural painkillers.

13. **insomnia**   In addition to this, getting physically tired can help people fall asleep faster and have deeper and more relaxing sleep. As many people suffering from anxiety often have problems with insomnia, just the ability to get a good night's rest can change people's whole perspectives.

14. **C**   Based upon the many foreign policy agreements Newfoundland had entered into prior to its admittance into the Canadian Confederation, foreign fleets, some from as far away as Russia, came to the Grand Banks in force, catching unprecedented quantities of fish.

15. **D**   It was during this time that it was noticed that the foreign fleets now pushed out to areas of the Grand Banks off Newfoundland outside the Canadian EEZ. By the late 1980's, dwindling catches of Atlantic cod were being reported throughout Newfoundland and eastern Canada, and the federal government and citizens of coastal regions in the area began to face the reality that the domestic and foreign overfishing had taken its toll.

16. **F**   However, earthquake and iceberg activity in the Grand Banks pose a potential ecological disaster that could devastate the fishing grounds that are only now starting to recover.

17. **A**   It is in this area that the cold Labrador Current mixes with the warm waters of the Gulf Stream. The mixing of these waters and the shape of the ocean bottom lifts nutrients to the surface and these conditions created one of the richest fishing grounds in the world.

18. **D**   On the whole, the EEZ was very well received by fishermen in eastern Canada

19. **E**   cod stocks are still only at approximately ten per cent of 1960's levels

20. **B**   The French pioneered 'wet' or 'green' fishery on the Grand Banks proper around 1550, heavily salting the cod on board and immediately returning home.

21. **C**   While the area's 'official' discovery is credited to John Cabot in 1497, English and Portuguese vessels are known to have first sought out these waters prior to that, based upon reports they received from earlier Viking voyages to Newfoundland.

22. **B**   However, it was not until John Cabot noted the waters' abundance of sea life that the existence of these fishing grounds became widely known in Europe.

23. **A**   It was during this time that it was noticed that the foreign fleets now pushed out to areas of the Grand Banks off Newfoundland outside the Canadian EEZ

24. **FALSE**   Either way, the early stage recovery of the Grand Banks is encouraging news, but caution is needed, as, after nearly twenty years of severe limitations, cod stocks are still only at approximately ten per cent of 1960's levels.

25. **TRUE**   The vast Hibernia oil field was discovered in 1979, and, following several years of aborted start-up attempts

26. **NOT GIVEN**   There is nothing in the text relating to this and so the answer is 'not given' in the text.

27. **longevity**   Population aging is driven by declines in fertility and improvements in health and longevity.

28. **less developed countries**   Perhaps the most surprising demographic development of the past 20 years has been the pace of fertility decline in many less developed countries.

29. **more developed nations**   Over several decades in the latter part of the 20th century, many of the more developed nations lowered the official age at which people become fully entitled to public pension benefits.

30. **reform**   Many countries already have taken steps towards much-needed reform of their old-age social insurance programs

31. **contributions**   One common reform has been to raise the age at which workers are eligible for full public pension benefits. Another strategy for bolstering economic security for older people has been to increase the contributions by workers.

32. **generations**   As life expectancy increases in most nations, so do the odds of different generations within a family coexisting. In more developed countries, this has manifested itself as the 'beanpole family,' a vertical extension of family structure characterised by an increase in the number of living generations within a lineage and a decrease in the number of people within each generation.

33. **(historical) precedent**   There is no historical precedent for a majority of middle-aged and older adults having living parents.

34. **NO**   The study estimates that today, non-communicable diseases account for 85 per cent of the burden of disease in high-income countries and a surprising 44 per cent of the burden of disease in low- and middle-income countries.

35. **NO**   The critical issue for low- and middle-income countries is how to mobilise and allocate resources to address non-communicable diseases, as they continue to struggle with the continued high prevalence of communicable diseases. Of course, a significant jump in disability numbers has accompanied the increase in longevity.

36. **YES**   Studies predict that, in the near term, surplus capital will flow from Europe and North America to emerging markets in Asia and Latin America, where the population is younger and cheaper and supplies of capital relatively low. In another 20 years, when the baby boom generation in the West has mostly retired, capital will most likely flow in the opposite direction.

37. **NOT GIVEN**   There is nothing in the text relating to this and so the answer is 'not given' in the text.

38. **YES**   Despite the weight of scientific evidence, the significance of population aging and its global implications have yet to be wholly appreciated.

39. **NO**   Experience shows that for nations, as for individuals, it is critical to address problems sooner rather than later. Waiting significantly increases the costs and difficulties of addressing these challenges.

40. **B**   This is a holistic answer and involves synthesis of the whole text. This text in its entirety fits the answer "To provide an overview of the causes and effects of the world's aging population" better than the other three answers.

ACADEMIC READING TEST 12

1. **FALSE**   A similar construction is the 'quinzhee', which is a shelter made by hollowing out a pile of settled snow, and is only for temporary use.

2. **NOT GIVEN**   There is nothing in the text relating to this and so the answer is 'not given' in the text.

3. **FALSE**   inside an igloo, the temperature may range from minus 7 degrees Celsius to 16 degrees Celsius when warmed by body heat alone.

4. **avalanche**   The first thing to do is to find a good spot. It is vital to choose a safe location away from avalanche prone slopes.

5. **stability**   Shovel a pile of snow into a large, reasonably steep mound and try and keep the sloping sides at an angle of around 35 degrees or higher, which is best for stability.

6. **temperatures**   If possible, mix snow of different temperatures to help it to harden.

7. **warm air**   Ideally, the floor of the snow shelter should be at least 30 centimetres above the entrance, which will help prevent warm air from escaping the shelter.

8. **dripping**   if the inside walls are smoothed, this will help prevent dripping.

9. **elevated**   Leave an elevated platform for sleeping on.

10. **(air) vent**   A very important point is to make an air vent in the wall of the shelter, which will prevent the occupants from suffocating in the night.

11. **(reindeer) hides**   In several winter destinations, villages of igloos are built for tourists, where the guests use sleeping bags that sit on top of reindeer hides in overnight stays.

12. **melt**   Ice hotels are found in many places in Norway, Finland, and Sweden, and are constructed each winter and melt in the spring.

13. **(interior) decorations**   It is made from the waters of the adjacent river Torne, the pure waters of which produce beautiful clear ice used to create interior decorations, which are made entirely of snow and ice.

14. **spread**   Worse than fire though, people may find that they cannot take their work elsewhere, for if they did, they might simply take the virus infection with them and bring more systems down.

15. **reputations**   Secondly, viruses can distribute disinformation and bring shame to individuals or organisations

16. **hide**   Successful viruses lie low until they have thoroughly infiltrated the system, and only reveal their presence when they cause damage.

17. **origins**   The effect of a virus is rarely linked back to its originator, so viruses make attractive weapons for vandals.

18. risks   A research virus is one that has been written for research or study purposes and has received almost no distribution to the public.

19. (Floppy) disks   Before the spread of the Internet, most computer viruses were spread by removable media, predominantly floppy disks.

20. (A) logic bomb   A logic bomb is a destructive program activated by a certain combination of circumstances, or on a certain date.

21. (A) worm   A worm is a distributed program that invades computers on a network. It consists of several processes or segments that keep in touch through the network; when one is lost, the others conspire to replace it on another server.

22. Mutation   Viruses today have no distinct identity, but typically undergo mutation each time they copy themselves to other files. This, combined with various cryptographic techniques, makes modern viruses difficult to detect.

23. Email   Email though has become the most popular way to disperse viruses today

24. variants   The majority of viruses are simple variants of others and many virus construction kits are readily available on the Internet.

25. (A) (regular) subscription   Because new viruses are being devised every day, it is important and sensible to keep detection programs up to date, by, for example, a regular subscription from a reputable firm

26. education of users   Eternal vigilance on the part of users is important, and, above all, education of users to the possible results of their actions.

27. E   In these ways, the school classroom, ideally, and the relations within it, is a model of some core aspects of citizenship.

28. C   Forming bonds and socialising with children his or her own age is important for a child's developmental health and development of social skills. If homeschooled, children may be deprived of the chance to form friendships and may suffer socially. The lack of socialisation may affect them in later stages of life.

29. G   Some children also have special abilities or needs, or simply idiosyncratic learning styles or habits, and many of these children can best or even only be educated by those who know them best.

30. A   or by using a company that specialises in providing homeschooling curricula and materials.

31. D   In comparison to public schools, where education is free, homeschooling can also be costly, as purchasing the newest curriculum and teaching tools can be very expensive.

32. F   The children are more susceptible to the diseases against which immunisation gives some protection, and others around them, particularly the elderly, are also consequently in danger.

33. **B**   Additionally, families can schedule off-season vacations

34. **A**   Homeschooled children can excel in standardised testing and universities and colleges have no qualms about accepting them.

35. **C**   Homeschooled children do not have to worry about bullying

36. **C**   They usually accomplish in a few hours each day what typically takes a week or more to complete in a classroom setting.

37. **B**   A more controversial benefit of homeschooling is that parents have frequently much more say in what is taught to their children, so that they can avoid subjects which they disapprove of.

38. **YES**   Parents choosing to homeschool their children may also be faced with the common problems of time and cost

39. **NO**   The unconditional love children receive at home is actually anything but unconditional: it is conditioned on the fact that they are their parents' children.

40. **NOT GIVEN**   There is nothing in the text relating to this and so the answer is 'not given' in the text.

ACADEMIC READING TEST 13

1. **ix**   Various information within Paragraph A.

2. **iii**   Various information within Paragraph B.

3. **vi**   Various information within Paragraph C.

4. **i**   Various information within Paragraph D.

5. **viii**   Various information within Paragraph E.

6. **x**   Various information within Paragraph F.

7. **iv**   Various information within Paragraph G.

8. **A***   Although the verified death toll was only six people

9. **C***   London had to be almost totally reconstructed and many people went to the fields outside London. They stayed there for many days, sheltering in tents and shacks and some people were forced to live in this way for months and even years.

10. **E***   this enabled the plague, which was common in London at that time, to spread easily.

11. **G***   As a result of the Great Fire of London, early fire brigades were formed by insurance companies.

12. **brick**   Houses now had to be faced in brick instead of wood.

13. **(brightly) (coloured) uniforms**   Also, fire fighters wore brightly coloured uniforms to distinguish themselves from rival insurance brigades.

14. **AH**   Andrea Haller, explains the state of the Yellowstone supervolcano. "By investigating the patterns of behaviour in two previously completed caldera cycles, we can suggest that the current activity of Yellowstone is on the dying cycle."

15. **AW**   Spokesman Alice Wheeler clarifies their position. "The scientist who first identified the three Yellowstone calderas was from the USGS and he told the world about the great eruptions that formed them. He traced out the caldera boundaries through old fashioned field work, walking around with a hammer and hand lens and looking carefully at the rocks and their distributions."

16. **GP**   Professor George Peters details the possible results if something were to happen. "A major eruption would obliterate the surroundings within a radius of hundreds of kilometres, and cover the rest of the United States and Canada with multiple inches of ash. This would shut down agriculture and cause global climate cooling for as long as a decade."

17. **JG**   Masters student, Julia Grey, explains the results. "By looking closely at data from thousands of earthquakes, we have discovered that there are two magma reservoirs, one shallow and one deep, and that they are much larger than originally believed.

18. **TM**   Tony Masters, explains there is little to fear today. "All VEI 8 eruptions, including the last at Yellowstone, occurred tens of thousands to millions of years ago.

19. **AB**   Yellowstone park scientist, Amy Brent, has calming words. "These findings do not increase the assessment of volcanic hazard for Yellowstone. The inferred magma storage region is no larger than we already knew. The research simply makes a better image of the magmatic system. Simply, we have more key information about how the Yellowstone volcano works."

20. **SF**   Stan Forsyth, their spokesman, explains. "Several authors have written that these large calderas in Yellowstone were discovered from space, but we suspect that the rumour probably got started because initial field work that identified them was partly funded by NASA."

21. **50**   The deeper magma storage region extends from 20 to 50 kilometres depth

22. **2%**   The deeper magma storage region extends from 20 to 50 kilometres depth, contains about 2 per cent melt, and is about 4.5 times larger than the shallow magma body.

23. **50%**   Although this is the crustal magma storage region that has fuelled Yellowstone's past volcanic activity, magma typically does not erupt unless it has greater than 50 per cent melt.

24. **A**   To create an image of this second magma reservoir beneath Yellowstone, the research teams reviewed data from thousands of earthquakes. Seismic waves travel slower through hot, partially molten rock and faster in cold, solid rock. The researchers made a map of the locations where seismic waves travel more slowly, which provided a sub-surface image of the hot or partially molten bodies in the crust beneath Yellowstone.

25. **C**   It is believed that Yellowstone is currently on a third and dying cycle. This can be concluded by the fact that dying volcanos produce less fresh molten material from the Earth's crust.

26. **A**   The park has often been closed due to volcanic activity in the past and this is likely to happen again before the volcano becomes harmless.

27. **(unconscious) barriers**   There are many people who have unconscious barriers that prevent them from having the wealth and abundance that they deserve.

28. **obsession**   Another problem is that, instead of focusing on all the possible ways to get rich, many people have an obsession about what they do not have.

29. **parent**   Alternatively, the person might have had a parent tell them over and over again that they will never be successful, and eventually they begin to believe it.

30. **YES**　　　　An imprint is basically a memory that is formed at an early age, and can serve as a root for both the limiting and empowering beliefs that people form as children. Some of the beliefs that people may develop at early ages are not always healthy, and are created as a result of a traumatic or confusing experience that they have forgotten. How we unconsciously and consciously view the world in terms of money is often based on such beliefs.

31. **NO**　　　　A primary and fundamental psychological difference between those who do well financially and those who do not revolves around beliefs.

32. **NO**　　　　They do not have the capability to open themselves up to all of the possibilities that are available for achieving prosperity and they will nearly always get stuck in a monthly routine, so that they are unwilling to take risks or try something different, because they are afraid that they will end up being even worse off than before.

33. **NOT GIVEN**　　　　There is nothing in the text relating to this and so the answer is 'not given' in the text.

34. **YES**　　　　It is most acute in those who inherit wealth and seem to have no purpose or direction.

35. **Diminishing returns**　　　　So, can money make people happy? Research shows that it does up to a point, after which there are diminishing returns, so that the extremely wealthy are no happier than the comfortably well off.

36. **factors**　　　　Rich nations are generally happier than poor ones, but the relationship is far from consistent; other factors like political stability, freedom and security also play a part.

37. **career satisfaction**　　　　Research likewise shows that the money-happiness connection seems to be stronger for people paid hourly than those on a salary. This is presumably because salaried people can more easily compensate with career satisfaction.

38. **simple things**　　　　Money can also impair the ability to enjoy the simple things in life, which rather offsets the happiness that wealth brings.

39. **(Cognitive) (dissonance) experiments**　　　　Money can also impair people's satisfaction in their play and humanitarian works. When someone has done something out of the goodness of their heart, they can be insulted by offers of payment. Cognitive dissonance experiments show that paying people derisory amounts of money for their work results in them enjoying it less and doing it less well than if they had no pay at all.

40. **(monetary) reward**　　　　The capacity for monetary reward to undermine a person's intrinsic pleasure in work performance has been demonstrated neurologically.

ACADEMIC READING TEST 14

1. **D**   Braille passed away in 1853 at the age of 43, a year before his home country of France adopted Braille as its official communication system for blind individuals.

2. **B**   The problem with the military code was that the human fingertip could not feel all the dots with one touch.

3. **G**   Today, Braille code is transcribed in many different languages worldwide.

4. **C**   One year earlier, he had enrolled at the National Institute of the Blind in Paris and he spent the next nine years developing and refining the system of raised dots that has come to be known by his name, Braille.

5. **E**   Once connected to the computer, the Braille display will acquire the currently highlighted text on the screen. The screen reader will then translate the text into Braille and the Braille display will display it on its built-in Braille cells.

6. **A**   Braille also contains equivalents for punctuation marks and provides symbols to show letter groupings.

7. **F**   As screen readers only let users hear the text on the screen, Braille displays are more useful for users who are both deaf and blind.

8. **(index) fingers**   Braille is read by moving the hand or hands from left to right along each line. Both hands are usually involved in the reading process, and reading is generally done with the index fingers.

9. **soldiers**   Charles Berbier developed a unique system known as 'night writing,' so that soldiers could communicate safely during the night.

10. **(phonetic) sound**   Berbier based his night writing system on a raised 12-dot cell; two dots wide and six dots tall. Each dot or combination of dots within the cell denoted a letter or a phonetic sound.

11. **awl**   Louis injured his eye with an awl. In spite of good care, infection set in and soon left him completely blind.

12. **contractions**   Braille codes for English and many other languages employ contractions that substitute shorter sequences for the full spelling of commonly occurring letter groups. For example, 'the' is usually just one character in Braille. The use of contractions permits faster Braille reading and helps reduce the size of Braille books, making them much less cumbersome.

13. **hardware**   Braille displays are hardware that enable users to read in Braille the text displayed on the computer screen.

14. **FALSE**   The singularity is a difficult thing to describe. It is not a place, but more where the curvature of space time is infinite. It is not known what goes on there, but it is known that it depends on quantum mechanics.

15. **TRUE**   Most famously, black holes were predicted by Einstein's theory of general relativity, which showed that, when a massive star dies, it leaves behind a small and dense remnant core.

16. **NOT GIVEN**   There is nothing in the text relating to this and so the answer is 'not given' in the text.

17. **TRUE**   Recent discoveries offer some evidence that black holes have a dramatic influence on things around them, emitting powerful gamma ray bursts, absorbing nearby stars, and both stimulating and hindering the growth of new stars.

18. **(The) photon sphere**   A static black hole has three things of particular interest. The outer part is known as the photon sphere, so named as photons orbit the black hole here.

19. **(The) singularity**   The centre of a black hole is the singularity and this where all the matter of a black hole from its origin lies, along with anything drawn in.

20. **electrocardiogram**   An international team of astronomers has identified a candidate for the smallest-known black hole using data from NASA's Rossi X-ray Timing Explorer (RXTE). The evidence comes from a specific type of X-ray pattern, nicknamed a 'heartbeat,' because of its resemblance to an electrocardiogram.

21. **mass**   The system in question combines a normal star with a black hole that may weigh less than three times the Sun's mass. That is, of course, near the theoretical mass boundary where black holes become possible.

22. **disk**   Gas from the normal star streams toward the black hole and forms a disk around it.

23. **(cyclical) variations**   Cyclical variations in the intensity of the X-rays observed reflect processes taking place within the gas disk.

24. **massive stars**   At the one end, there are the countless black holes that are the remnants of massive stars.

25. **isolated**   Most stellar black holes, however, lead isolated lives and are impossible to detect.

26. **all large galaxies**   Astronomers believe that supermassive black holes lie at the middle of virtually all large galaxies.

27. **A***   In addition, it appears from the research that CCTV is effective in addressing property crime and some types of assault and robbery.

28. **C***   Of course, high-risk areas, for example jewellery shops, can greatly benefit from the visible deterrent of CCTV cameras.

29. **F***   people believe CCTV brings can lead to enhanced perceptions of safety in a particular area, which makes communities happier and more satisfied with government actions.

30. **crime problem**   In general, the issue of whether or not to consider implementing a CCTV scheme is likely to arise in response to a perception or awareness that there is a crime problem in a specific public place.

31. **(local) council**   Once a local council identifies that there is a problem, it needs to form a Community Safety Committee

32. **co-ordinator**   Alternatively, a program co-ordinator with experience in developing community safety initiatives could be appointed to manage the development of the CCTV program.

33. **(local) police**   The analysis should be conducted in consultation with local police, and, as appropriate, representatives of the local community.

34. **Crime Prevention Plan**   Once the crime assessment provides a clear picture of the nature of the criminal activities, a Crime Prevention Plan should be made.

35. **appropriate**   If the Committee believes that one of the strategies to address the problems identified in the crime assessment is the establishment of a CCTV program, it is essential that the Crime Prevention Plan outlines how this strategy is integrated with the broad plan objectives and why CCTV is considered appropriate.

36. **surveillance (apparatus)**   It is argued that the steady expansion in the surveillance apparatus of the state and private sector has diminished the privacy of every individual, has lessened people's trust in the state and poses a significant threat to personal privacy and individual freedom.

37. **unconstitutional**   Although in most countries there is nothing inherently unconstitutional in the use of surveillance by the state, there is nonetheless a danger that it may disturb some of the presumptions and relationships that underpin the relationship between the individual and the state.

38. **discrimination**   There are also worries about the social effects of surveillance and the potential for discrimination. Cameras are installed so as to watch places and identified groups of people.

39. **(institutional) biases**   Studies have shown that existing surveillance systems and databases with collected information may reflect institutional biases, often based on factors such as race.

40. **(rigorous) evaluation**   Therefore, as CCTV on its own can do little to address long-term crime prevention, CCTV should only be considered as one part of an integrated crime prevention strategy and should be installed on a trial basis subject to rigorous evaluation as to its usefulness.

ACADEMIC READING TEST 15

1. **B***   The iconic waterway established settlement patterns for most of the United States during the nineteenth century, made New York the financial capital of the world

2. **D***   The iconic waterway established settlement patterns for most of the United States during the nineteenth century, made New York the financial capital of the world, provided a critical supply line that helped the North win the Civil War

3. **F***   influential Senator De Witt Clinton, former mayor of New York City, to enlist his support. Though Clinton had been recruited to the canal effort by Eddy and Platt, he quickly became one of the canal's most active supporters and went on to successfully tie his very political fate to its success.

4. **H***   The explosion of trade prophesied by Governor Clinton began, spurred by freight rates from Buffalo to New York of $10 per ton by canal, compared with $100 per ton by road.

5. **I***   nearly 80 per cent of upstate New York's inhabitants live within 25 miles of the Erie Canal.

6. **K***   Today, the canal has returned to its former glory and is filled with pleasure boats, fishermen, holidaymakers and cyclists riding the former towpaths where mules once trod.

7. **(Sluice) gates**   Locks have two sets of sluice gates (top and bottom), which seal off and then open the entrances to the chamber

8. **(The) chamber**   by opening these valves that water is allowed into and out of the chamber to raise or lower the water level, and hence the boat.

9. **Valves**   locks also have valves at the bottom of the sluice gates and it is by opening these valves

10. **Fertile land**   The Northwest Territories that would later become Illinois, Indiana, Michigan and Ohio were rich in timber, minerals, and fertile land for farming, but it took weeks to reach these things.

11. **Flour**   An imprisoned flour merchant named Jesse Hawley envisioned a better way

12. **8 years**   Construction began on July 4th 1817 and took eight years.

13. **(Canal) tolls**   In nine years, canal tolls more than recouped the entire cost of construction

14. **ix**   Various information within Paragraph A.

15. **iv**   Various information within Paragraph B.

16. **vi**   Various information within Paragraph C.

17. **i**   Various information within Paragraph D.

Page 135

18. **v**   Various information within Paragraph E.

19. **iii**   Various information within Paragraph F.

20. **viii**   Various information within Paragraph G.

21. **A**   Opium has a very bitter taste that is comparable to other plants from similar families and a distinct odour that is clearly identifiable.

22. **C**   The history of opium dates back as far as the Neolithic and ancient times, when the drug was widely used in anaesthesia

23. **D**   However, for some, the effects of opium use are dangerous almost immediately

24. **selective breeding**   Overall, opium production has changed very little over the years, however, selective breeding of the plant has led to an increase in the content of the phenanthrene alkaloids morphine, codeine and thebaine.

25. **Chinese**   It was nearly 300 years before the Chinese first realised that smoking opium was actually dangerous and could lead to physical dependence.

26. **Counselling**   Most of the time, inpatient or residential treatment will be the basis for recovery. These programs will utilise counselling in both individual and group sessions to provide a foundation for success in recovery.

27. **FALSE**   For quite some time now, video games that involve significant amounts of violence have been blamed for growing numbers of violence by young people, the demographic most likely to play these games.

28. **TRUE**   Some experts involved have proclaimed that the debate is scientifically settled and that only people holding personal concerns and biases oppose these established truths.

29. **FALSE**   Studies suggest that at-risk individuals are usually male

30. **TRUE**   Another recent key report which relied on parents' self-report of their children's video game–playing behaviours suggests that spending a large amount of time playing violent video games was correlated with troublesome behaviour and poor academic achievement.

31. **NOT GIVEN**   There is nothing in the text relating to this and so the answer is 'not given' in the text.

32. **TRUE**   In 1954, the US Senate Subcommittee on Juvenile Delinquency held hearings on the effects of comic books on America's youth. The primary focus of the Senate hearings was 'crime and horror' comic books, some of which graphically showed horrific images, such as dismembered bodies.

33. **TRUE**   Many of the concerns that dominate the current video game debate were also expressed and it could show the frequently experienced perception that violent behaviour is always more prevalent in the present than in the past and that people just search for a scapegoat on which to blame it.

34. **(mental) wellness scores**   One study in fact showed that non-gamers and excessive gamers both had lower self-reported mental wellness scores than low to moderate gamers.

35. **aggression**   This finding is in line with social theory, which suggests that video games, like sports, may provide an outlet for individuals to work through aggression and, therefore, have better mental functioning and overall lower levels of aggression.

36. **decision-making (capabilities)**   The same study pointed to the positive attributes of violent video game playing, such as improved visual-spatial coordination, increased peripheral attention, and increased decision-making capabilities.

37. **neighbourhood (quality)**   The factors that were not found to be predictive of youth violence included neighbourhood quality, parental use of domestic physical violence in intimate relationships, and exposure to violent television or video games.

38. **brain imaging**   A recent neurological study provided further evidence that video games do not increase violent behaviour by users. The study examined whether there was a change in brain imaging that suggested a loss of distinction between virtual and actual violence in players of violent video games compared with controls.

39. **desensitisation (processes)**   What was found was that the ability to differentiate automatically between real and virtual violence was not diminished by a long-term history of violent video game play, and nor were gamers' neural responses to real violence subject to desensitisation processes.

40. **D**   This is a holistic answer and involves synthesis of the whole text. This text in its entirety fits the answer "To review what has been discovered about the effects of violent video games" better than the other three answers.

EXAMPLE WRITING ANSWERS

Below you will find example writing answers for all the writing questions in the Academic Practice Tests 11 to 15. There are many ways of answering the writing questions and these examples are only one possibility of a good answer. Please refer to the question papers while you are reading these reports and essays so that you understand the questions that are being answered. We hope this will give you an insight into how the writing answers should be written for IELTS Academic module.

ACADEMIC WRITING PRACTICE TEST 11

Task 1

This report concerns a bar chart, which compares Scotland's exports in different areas of industry to the rest of the UK with its exports to the rest of the world in 2014.

In general, Scotland exports more to the rest of the world than to the rest of the UK in all the industries mentioned with one exception. The Electrical & Instrument Engineering industry exports are £4 billion to the rest of the UK compared to £2.3 billion going to the rest of the world.

In other industry sectors, the difference in exports is most significant in the Business Services & Finance, Hotels & Restaurant Services Industry with exports to the rest of the world worth £13.8 billion and exports to the UK worth only £1.7 billion. Other significant sectors are Chemicals & Mineral Products and the Wholesale & Retail industries.

In conclusion, exports to the rest of the world are clearly more significant to the Scottish economy than those to the rest of the UK.   (166 words)

Task 2

The pressure exerted onto children nowadays is immense. Not only are many schools transformed into all-days establishments, but for many children the end of school is not the end of their day. Parents often organise extra classes for their children after school and at the weekends to educate their children further. It is argued that this is unnecessary pressure, as children have enough education at school.

In most schools, children are educated in the sciences, languages and mathematics, as well as physical education and the arts. This wide range of subjects is aimed at creating a well-rounded student. Due to this variety, extra classes are unnecessary, as the student can adequately learn to be exposed to all different aspects of education. Furthermore, additional classes can lead to stressed children that are incapable of performing well in school, as they lack time to really comprehend and practice the knowledge learned. Therefore, extra classes can actually lead to students performing worse in school, as the students cannot fully grasp any knowledge that they learn, whether in school or in the extra classes.

However, in some schools the range is not as developed as it should be or the level that they are at is not sufficient for a student. In this case it does make sense to further educate children outside of school. Whether the extra classes have positive or negative effects depends solely on the child and how they perform in school.

In conclusion, extra classes can be helpful to some students who are not challenged enough in school. Parents should be careful about deciding whether their children need the extra help or whether free time for playing and relaxation might be more beneficial.   (283 words)

ACADEMIC WRITING PRACTICE TEST 12

Task 1

This report refers to two bar charts. The first gives data on obesity in boys by ethnicity between the ages of twelve and nineteen in the United States for 2004 and 2014 and the second gives the same data for girls.

In boys, the obesity figures for 2004 were similar for all three ethnicities given, at 12, 11 and 13 per cent for Non-Hispanic White, Non-Hispanic Black and Hispanic respectively. In 2014, these figures rose to 17, 20 and 27 per cent for the same ethnicities. All these figures for 2014 are high, especially the last with over a quarter of this age group being classed as obese.

In girls, the obesity figures for 2004 were similar to boys for Non-Hispanic White and Hispanic, at 9 and 12 per cent respectively. The figure for Non-Hispanic Black was significantly higher for girls at 16 per cent. In 2014, Non-Hispanic White and Hispanic both rose 5 per cent and remained less than their male counterparts. Non-Hispanic Black girls, however, rose to 29 per cent, which is the highest figure in both charts.

In conclusion, the obesity figures shown for the US are extremely worrying, especially for the Non-Hispanic Black demographic.   *(198 words)*

Task 2

In current society, the life expectancy in western countries has increased significantly. Also, fewer babies are being born, causing the relative percentage of elderly people to increase. These people have to be taken care of, causing the question to rise whether this number of elderly people can be cared for.

When people grow older, they can also develop more health issues, resulting in more visits to doctors and hospitals, and an increased usage of pharmaceuticals. Due to the current large numbers of elderly people, the pressure put onto health care systems is increasing. In many western countries, the state provides most of the health care system. Therefore with increasing numbers of old people, higher percentages of state funding have to be allocated to health care and this could cause shortfalls in other areas, for example education. This change in the distribution of money can therefore impact society negatively.

Society should be able to handle these changes. Governments will have been able to predict the changing demographic situations in their countries and plan accordingly. This might indeed lead to other sectors in society having money taken away from them, but caring for the elderly is one of the key responsibilities of today's governments. For the future, it might be necessary to ensure that an extra insurance charge is levied on people's salaries in order that any future financial shortfall is met. This would be unpopular, but would allow governments to have the necessary funds available.

In conclusion, society today and in the future should be well able to deal with caring for their elderly. It is only a question of careful long-term forecasting and planning.   *(274 words)*

ACADEMIC WRITING PRACTICE TEST 13

Task 1

This graph shows the amount of money tourists from five different countries spent while visiting New Zealand for the years 1996 to 2014. The five countries compared are Australia, the USA, the UK, Japan and China. In 1996, the order of countries whose citizens spent the most was as follows: Australia, USA, Japan, UK, and China. In 2014, the only change was that Japan and the UK had switched places.

The amount of money spent in New Zealand by tourists from all the named countries increased from 1996 to 2014, although there were some minor fluctuations. The visitor expenditure that increased the most was for visitors from Australia. In 1996, Australian tourists were spending around NZ$1000, a value which had doubled by 2014, with a peak of NZ$2500 in 2006.

The expenditure of Chinese tourists in New Zealand in 1996 was negligible, reflecting that New Zealand was not an attractive destination to the Chinese people at the time. However by 2014, the expenditure had increased to around NZ$400, after having reached a peak of NZ$500 in 2004, suggesting that New Zealand had become a more attractive destination to the citizens of China.   *(192 words)*

Task 2

In nearly every city around the world, the volume of traffic on roads has become a significant problem. Society's dependence on the car has led to nearly all families owning at least one car and often two. Changing this situation will not be easy, but a series of social reforms and education could allow the numbers of cars on today's roads to be reduced.

To decrease traffic, multiple social reforms could be imposed. First of all, fuel prices could be raised, while simultaneously public transportation improved. The aim would be to make more people rely on public transportation. Another method to decrease traffic in cities would be to decrease the number of parking slots in the city and increase the cost for these. This method also aims at encouraging the usage of public transportation, as it would make public transport more appealing than parking. Another social reform could be to give tax breaks, if proven, that the person is using public transport on a regular basis.

In addition to social reforms, each individual would need to be educated to increase awareness of the environment. This could be achieved through addressing the matter using multiple media. Within this campaign, the environmental as well as the individual benefits of decreasing the usage of cars would have to be highlighted.

In conclusion, only when individuals become aware can social reforms function properly. Success would mean more people using public transport and fewer people using cars. When this goal is achieved, stress on the environment will be decreased.   *(254 words)*

ACADEMIC WRITING PRACTICE TEST 14

Task 1

The bar chart gives data on the top ten processed food export markets for the United States from last year and six years ago.

The largest market by far for last year and six years ago was Canada with income for the US of 13.2 billion US dollars and 9.3 billion US dollars respectively. The second highest figures were for what is identified as the Rest of World at 11 billion US dollars and 6.3 billion US dollars respectively.

The remaining eight countries ranged from Mexico with income for the US of 6.1 billion US dollars for last year and 4 billion US dollars for six years ago to Hong Kong with income for the US of 0.8 billion US dollars for last year and 0.3 billion US dollars for six years ago. Therefore the two largest markets the US depends on for their processed food exports were the closest ones, Canada and Mexico.

Notable features are that all countries in the bar chart had higher figures for last year than six years ago, and that most countries importing US processed foods, the exceptions being Canada, Mexico and the Rest of the World, were all across the Pacific from the US. All these countries are Asian, except for Australia. Asian markets together are therefore vital for the US processed food industry.   *(221 words)*

Task 2

Banning cars from city centres is a recent trend and it can be seen in various cities around the world. Certain advantages and disadvantages immediately spring to mind when considering this step that city councils are taking.

The advantages are clear. Since cars were introduced, city centres have always been areas where air quality is poor due to the amount of emissions, which in turn affects people's health. City centres become quieter and safer for people to wander around shopping and enjoying themselves. Access to city centres can still be good, as it is usually only private vehicles that are banned, and buses and taxis can still take people in and out of the city centre areas. Many towns also operate a park and ride scheme, so people can leave their cars in safe car parks in the outskirts of towns and travel with a dedicated bus service to the town centres. It would seem hard to criticise this kind of scheme.

There are critics though to the scheme of banning cars in city centres. City centre shop keepers have often been vocal opponents, as they believe that fewer people will come to the city centres and therefore their incomes will be affected. The general public also sometimes object, as people often like to travel in their own private vehicles. In actual fact, banning cars from city centres has in practice not reduced the number of people who travel to city centres to shop. People like shopping and socialising in city centres and they just adapt to the situation. There is no answer to people who want to drive their own cars. They hopefully will just realise that the sacrifice of not driving their own cars is outweighed by the health and lifestyle improvements of a cleaner and quieter city centre.

In conclusion, there are far more and more significant advantages to banning cars from city centres than allowing them. It is therefore a measure that most city centres should adopt for their citizens. *(334 words)*

Page 141

ACADEMIC WRITING PRACTICE TEST 15

Task 1

Both of the flow charts describe circles of poverty, however, they look at them from different perspectives. The first flow chart looks at poverty from an institutional level, while the second looks at it from the perspective of an individual.

The first flow chart explains how poverty results in the lack of a critical mass for service and infrastructure, which can lead to lower business creation. This in turn leads to fewer jobs and the moving away of workers, so they can find a job elsewhere. If workers begin to move away, then the population density of the cities decreases, which then again influences the lack of a mass needed for the infrastructure. And so the circle continues.

The second flow chart looks at the more personal hardships of poverty, starting with low income, low assets and low education in an individual. Low education leads to a lack of skills and a lack of capital, which makes it even harder for an individual to generate income. This provides an individual with only a low security against economic and health risks and can lead to debt and a further loss of income.

(191 words)

Task 2

To perform well in a job, people have to be motivated. There are multiple strategies for employers to motivate their employees. The most obvious one is the salary, however, job satisfaction and the ability to help people are other methods of motivation.

For the majority of the people, receiving their salary at the end of the month is their motivation. This is because money is necessary to fulfill the most basic needs and other materialistic desires. People see these opportunities when receiving their salary and therefore work to achieve money. Furthermore, performing well in a job can often lead to promotions with higher salaries. To receive this, people have to stand out positively in their jobs. Salary is therefore a key motivational tool for many people.

However, money is not the only method of motivation. Another aspect affecting performance is job satisfaction. If a person is comfortable in their work, they are more likely to perform well. Therefore this motivational tool interlinks with salary, as when people are content and perform well, the chances of promotion increase. For some people though, only their passion can drive them. Prime examples for this are humanitarian jobs. The salaries are often not very high, but the people working in this area are often very driven; their passion to help other people is prioritised over their own salary.

In conclusion, while salary might be the most common motivational factor, it is unusual to be the sole incentive for working hard, and some people are motivated wholly due to other reasons.

(256 words)

COMMENTARY ON THE EXAMPLE SPEAKING RECORDINGS

In this section you will find reports by an IELTS speaking examiner on the recordings of
Speaking Tests 11 - 15. The questions asked in the recordings are the questions in the Speaking Tests 11 – 15, so, while listening to the recordings, it is advised to have the questions with you for reference. The recordings are not real IELTS test recordings, but the interviewer is a real IELTS examiner and the recordings are conducted in the exact way that an IELTS Speaking Test is done.

SPEAKING PRACTICE TEST 11

Examiner's Commentary

The person interviewed is Pedro, a Chilean male. Pedro is a teacher.

Section 1

Pedro spoke very fluently and accurately. He has a very slight accent, but his accent often seems to be more American than Chilean. He spoke calmly, and with humour and intelligence. Pedro's vocabulary range is very strong and he rarely needs to pause to access the right word. There were very few errors, though there were occasional inconsistencies ("it's played along the year" instead of 'all through the year')

Section 2

Pedro had no problems with speaking for the longer section. He again spoke fluently and accurately with his negligible Chilean accent. His vocabulary range was extremely good, with no apparent problems.

Section 3

Pedro again gave measured and full answers. He was accurate, fluent and clear. His pronunciation was again very good, with his American accent clearly apparent. He did use some slightly different intonation, which made some words sound a little different to how a native speaker would pronounce them. There were no particular grammar or word choice problems.

Marking - The marking of the IELTS Speaking Test is done in 4 parts.

Fluency and Coherence	9
Lexical Resource	9
Grammatical Range and Accuracy	9
Pronunciation	8
Estimated IELTS Speaking Band	**9**

SPEAKING PRACTICE TEST 12

Examiner's Commentary

The person interviewed is Kuba, a Polish male. Kuba is a professional diver.

Section 1

Kuba spoke fairly fluently and generally accurately. Kuba had a good answer for all the questions, but there were certain limitations in his vocabulary and grammar range and he often had to pause to access language and sometimes tailed off. This led to fairly short answers for some of the questions. Quite often though, Kuba did show that he knew some more unusual lexis, probably due to the time that he spent in the US, which he mentioned in section 2. Kuba's accent was quite strong, but did not really affect communication.

Section 2

Kuba spoke well and confidently in this section. He still had some limitations in vocabulary and grammar and he also made occasional errors (i.e. "I used to work as a card dealer in casino" instead of "I used to work as a card dealer in a casino"). This error was typical for him, as he made quite a few article errors, which often happens with Slavic languages. Kuba lacked a little fluency in places and at one time he had to stop, as he could not access the word "environment" (a word he remembered just after the test stopped).

Section 3

The more demanding nature of the questions in section 3 led to Kuba making shorter and sometimes less fluent answers here, although he also gave some good and long answers. The grammar and vocabulary range were reasonable, but again there was a lack of range that showed Kuba's limitations.

Marking - The marking of the IELTS Speaking Test is done in 4 parts.

Fluency and Coherence	6
Lexical Resource	6
Grammatical Range and Accuracy	6
Pronunciation	7

Estimated IELTS Speaking Band   **6**

SPEAKING PRACTICE TEST 13

Examiner's Commentary

The person interviewed is Deniz, a Turkish female. Deniz is a graphic designer.

Section 1

Deniz spoke fluently and confidently. She used vocabulary and grammar flexibly and accurately and has the ability to use longer and complex sentences without difficulty. She speaks with an accent, but this is not intrusive. There were occasional errors ("more green" instead of "greener" or "but if it is a grocery" or "it might help you to growth" instead of "grow"), but these did not affect communication. Deniz also uses English in a colloquial way at appropriate times, which makes her sound very comfortable with using English. There were occasional pauses as she accessed vocabulary, but she interacted well with the examiner to ensure that she was understood.

Section 2

Deniz chose a good subject for her section 2. It was a famous place and allowed her to talk at length. She spoke a long time, in spite of the fact that she speaks quite quickly. Again her vocabulary, grammar and general communicative ability were very good. There were again errors ("Once in a year" instead of "once a year"), but again these did not impede communication. Deniz's accent was still apparent, but she spoke clearly and the occasional word or phrase seemed by her pronunciation that she has spent some time in a native English-speaking country.

Section 3

Deniz gave long and complex answers for section 3 and showed she had the language ability to discuss more complex ideas. It helped that she had studied architecture, but this does not necessarily mean that she would have the vocabulary range in English that she clearly has. Again, all aspects of Deniz's English were very good.

Marking - The marking of the IELTS Speaking Test is done in 4 parts.

Fluency and Coherence	7
Lexical Resource	7
Grammatical Range and Accuracy	7
Pronunciation	8

Estimated IELTS Speaking Band   **7**

SPEAKING PRACTICE TEST 14

Examiner's Commentary

The person interviewed is Shaifali, a Singaporean female. Shaifali is a student.

Section 1

Right from the start, Shaifali showed that she had an excellent command of English; she spoke fluently, confidently and idiomatically. Shaifali gave full and intelligent answers to all questions and did not hesitate to access language or structure. Shaifali's grammar was very accurate and there were no errors. Her word choice was also automatic and highly appropriate in all speeches. Shaifali did not seem to have any interference in her accent at all from a mother tongue. Shaifali also used humour in appropriate situations.

Section 2

Shaifali showed again section 2 her strong ability in English and she had no problem speaking at length. Although an extremely strong candidate, she still took the whole minute available to prepare her talk, which is always highly advisable. Shaifali spoke fluently and again with humour and showed that she could perform a long turn without any problems at all. Again her vocabulary and grammar ranges were excellent and she did not make any errors at all.

Section 3

The greater demands of section 3 only allowed Shaifali to show her excellent standard of English. She spoke sensitively and coherently with the more difficult questions, without any errors coming into her English. Her pronunciation remained impeccable and of a native speaker standard.

Marking - The marking of the IELTS Speaking Test is done in 4 parts.

Fluency and Coherence	9
Lexical Resource	9
Grammatical Range and Accuracy	9
Pronunciation	9
Estimated IELTS Speaking Band	**9**

SPEAKING PRACTICE TEST 15

Examiner's Commentary

The person interviewed is Teresita, a Philippine female. Teresita is a nurse.

Section 1

Teresita spoke very fluently and confidently. Her speech was very clear and her accent was hardly apparent. Her sentences were well constructed and her lexis were varied and reasonably idiomatic. There were some grammar errors with article problems being apparent. Occasionally there were some grammar and lexis problems with sentences carrying some wrong or awkward choices (e.g.: "that their team had that loss). Teresita's answers were fairly full and she was good at adding detail to her comments.

Section 2

Teresita underperformed in this section. She spoke only for 30 seconds and the examiner had to prompt her to address some of the questions on the card. Teresita did not use her minute's preparation and seemed over-confident. By not reading what was required of her, she did not speak for long enough and did not show her English abilities. What English she did produce showed again that she was a strong English user, though she did make some errors.

Section 3

A good performance here, though Teresita still showed that she has problems with articles. She showed her good vocabulary and grammar range. Teresita still needed to develop answers a bit more fully, as it sometimes gave the impression that she did not have the language to do so. This resulted in section 3 being a little shorter than it should have been. At the end, Teresita did not clearly listen to the question. When asked how education prepares young people for technology today, Teresita talked about how young people need to learn when to use their phones.

Marking - The marking of the IELTS Speaking Test is done in 4 parts.

Fluency and Coherence	7
Lexical Resource	7
Grammatical Range and Accuracy	7
Pronunciation	8
Estimated IELTS Speaking Band	**7**

Listening Recordings' Transcripts

LISTENING TEST 11 TRANSCRIPT

This recording is copyright.

IELTS-Blog.com listening practice tests. Test eleven. In the IELTS test you hear some recordings and you have to answer questions on them. You have time to read the instructions and questions and check your work. All recordings are played only once. The test is in four sections. Now turn to section one.

Section one. You will hear a conversation between a man and a woman as the woman buys a new bus pass.

First you have some time to look at questions one to five.

(20 second gap)

You will see that there is an example. This time only, the conversation relating to this will be played first.

David	Good morning, Madam. How can I help you?
Louise	Hi there. My name's Louise. I need to get a new bus pass.
David	Do you know which zones you'll need it for?
Louise	Yes. Zones one, two and three.

So, three is the correct answer.

Now the full test will begin. You should answer the questions as you listen, as the recording is not played twice. Listen carefully to the conversation and answer questions one to five.

David	Good morning, Madam. How can I help you?
Louise	Hi there. My name's Louise. I need to get a new bus pass.
David	Do you know which zones you'll need it for?
Louise	Yes. Zones one, two and <u>three</u>.
David	That's fine. Now, have you had a bus pass before?
Louise	Yes, I've had one for the last <u>six months</u> and it expired today.
David though.	That's good. I won't need to take your details then. I'll need to confirm some information
Louise	That's fine.
David	Can you let me know your postcode?

Page 149

Louise	It's NW thirteen, four SG.
David	And can you let me know the number of the house at that postcode?
Louise	It's number thirteen.
David still right?	I've got your records here. It says that we should contact you on your mobile phone. Is that
Louise address.	I'd like to change that actually to <u>email</u>. I've not changed it, so you should have my current
David	Let's see. Is it louise k at UK net dot com?
Louise	That's right.
David	OK. I've made a note of that.
Louise	I won't get extra spam, will I?
David or contact you without good reason.	No, don't worry. Our data policy specifies that we can't pass on your information to anyone
Louise	Good. Thank you.
David have a photo with you?	Now on your old bus pass, there was no <u>photo</u>. The new one will be a photocard. Do you
Louise	No, I don't. I didn't know that I would need it.
David I can take it here if you like. Just look at this screen.	That's OK. We put the requirement on the website, but of course most people don't see it.
Louise	Like this?
David	That's right. Now keep still. OK. That's done.
Louise	By the way, is the price still a hundred pounds?
David	I'm afraid not. The price went up by <u>five per cent</u>. It's still pretty good value though.
Louise	Yes. That's fine.
David	So, here's your new pass and here's a new holder. I saw that your old one had got bit worn.
Louise bottom of my bag all the time.	Yes, it had. Thanks very much. The old one had gotten a bit beaten up, being at the
David valid without it, so you'd better do that now to your new one.	One more thing. I noticed there was no <u>signature</u> on the back of your old bus pass. It isn't

Louise   Oh, I didn't know that either. I'll do it now. There you are.

Before the conversation continues, you have some time to look at questions six to ten.

(20 second gap)

Now listen carefully and answer questions six to ten.

David   Is there anything else I can help you with?

Louise   Yes, there is actually. You know that all the bus routes have been reorganised recently.

David   Yes.

Louise   Well, I'm a bit confused. Could you briefly explain some of the changes?

David   Of course. First of all, there is route one. That's the one that goes in the direction of the town hospital when it goes north and the university when it goes south. There are two bus stops where you can get on this. To go north, you need to find bus stop Q. That's on Alton Road, just outside the town hall. To go south, towards the university, then find bus stop P, which is also on Alton Road, outside the cinema.

Louise   That's useful for me, as I study at the university. Now I live in West Howe. What will I need to do to get a route one bus?

David   The best way is to go to the town centre and change. You'll need to take route three. Take the bus from the centre of West Howe and get off at the town centre at bus stop G. That's outside West Gate Shopping Centre. Then, to get back to West Howe, you'll need to go back to West Gate Shopping Centre and find bus stop H, opposite bus stop G.

Louise   Thanks. Finally, I need to know how to get to the Arrowdown Sports Centre. I was given a membership there and so I'll be going there quite often too.

David   First of all, you need to come to the centre of town, as you would normally. Then to get to that sports centre, you'll need to go to the town centre post office. The buses for the Arrowdown Centre are from bus stop A. To get back, take the bus from outside the sports centre and get off at bus stop C in the town centre.

Louise   Thanks for that. Now, a friend told me that I can get discounts using my bus pass. He said that I can get cheaper cinema tickets and train tickets with it.

David   I'm afraid not with the cinema, but you'll get a fifteen per cent discount on local train services. There are other possibilities as well. The local football club gives you access to the special hospitality area, although you'll need to buy a regular ticket. You can also get priority seating at the local theatre and the local museum gives bus pass holders cheaper entry. Some of these things are restricted by availability, of course.

Louise   Well, that's a bonus!

Page 151

That is the end of section one. You will now have half a minute to check your answers.

(30 second gap)

Now turn to section two.

Section two. You will hear a man giving an information talk at an adult education centre. First you have some time to look at questions eleven to fifteen.

(20 second gap)

Now listen carefully to the information talk and answer questions eleven to fifteen.

Good evening everyone and thanks for coming to this information evening at the Adult Education Centre. My name is Mike and I'll be speaking to you for a short while before you can go and explore the various departments that we have here.

The centre was founded fifty years ago by <u>the town council</u> in order to help people who had failed to get a proper education when they were children. The idea today is a little different. We can give people the chance to study what they missed at school for whatever reason, but we can also just give them training in everyday skills or just allow them to extend themselves.

The teachers in the centre are fully qualified and their teaching is appraised <u>every six months</u> by inspectors from the Ministry of Education. Our teachers have the latest teaching aids and accessories, from interactive whiteboards to computer labs with the most up-to-date technology. All our teachers undergo special training and all their lessons can be found online at what we call <u>the interactive classroom</u>, which is accessible by all registered students. All notes, videos and worksheets can be found there, so if you miss a lesson, you can catch up on your computer at home. As well as just finding the resources, you can be in direct contact with your teacher. Naturally, he or she cannot be online all day, but every teacher has two online tutorial sessions of <u>three hours</u> each when they are available to chat. They can of course be in demand, so they are limited to four students at any one time and students can only interact with their teacher for a maximum of ten minutes. If the teacher is free though, students may continue to chat for longer.

Naturally, we also have a normal website. This has details of all our courses, teachers, fees and timetables. All courses can be booked and paid for online, although you'll need of course to supply credit card or bank account details. If you don't want to book online, you'll need to come to our main centre on Langdon Street between the hours of ten a.m. and <u>two p.m.</u>, which are the hours that our administration section is open to the general public.

You now have some time to look at questions sixteen to twenty.

(20 second gap)

Now listen to the rest of the information talk and answer questions sixteen to twenty.

Page 152

Now let me tell you a little about the courses that we have on offer. I'll begin with languages, as they're often very popular. We offer a variety of European languages, including French, German, Polish and Spanish. In addition, we offer Arabic, Korean, Japanese and Mandarin Chinese. These languages are offered at various stages of ability and to find out which class you belong in, you can do our <u>self-assessment test</u> available on our website for all the languages we offer.

Next, I'd like to tell you about our business related courses. Our business courses vary from short morning or afternoon sessions, where you will develop an excellent understanding of a particular topic, to courses that run for over thirty weeks, where you can achieve an industry-recognised qualification. From learning how to use essential computer software to <u>bookkeeping</u> or search engine optimisation and website development, we have the business courses to help you achieve your goals. These courses are always the most popular, so if you're interested, make sure you make your booking fast. We only take ten people per course and these places go quickly.

One of our most popular course areas is photography and <u>computers for photography</u>. Our range of courses on these subjects can help you learn to get the most out of your camera. From basic to advanced, our courses will allow you to build up your knowledge and learn new ways to use your equipment.

Another favourite are our cooking courses. We offer speciality courses, but a favourite is our introduction to cooking. This course is ideal for those new to cooking or for anyone wishing to create achievable and inspiring dishes. Learn a variety of essential cooking techniques to help you create simple everyday dishes or some more elaborate things to impress your guests. You will also learn to make the best use of store cupboard ingredients, and how to take delicious <u>shortcuts</u> to make cooking quick and enjoyable every day.

I'll finish with telling you about our creative writing course. It looks at practical ways to get started, whilst promoting greater writing confidence. The focus of this course is placed on practical exercises supported by discussion and examples and builds upon the strengths of each writer. It will give you an insight into the creative process and encourage you to achieve your writing goals. Our creative writing course provides an opportunity for all aspiring writers to develop the <u>skills</u> for writing fiction.

We have lots more courses and I urge you to check our website, as we don't have enough time to introduce everything that we have on offer.

That is the end of section two. You will now have half a minute to check your answers.

(30 second gap)

Now turn to section three.

Section three. You will hear four students discussing a survey that they will conduct. First you have some time to look at questions twenty-one to twenty-six.

(20 second gap)

Now listen carefully and answer questions twenty-one to twenty-six.

Page 153

Abbie	Hi Martin. Hi Rachel. Are you both waiting for us?
Martin	Hi Abbie. Hi Lance. Yes, we are, but we've not been waiting long.
Rachel	Yes. We just ordered some coffee. Hi Lance.
Lance	Hi everyone.

Martin   So, we're here today to talk about our survey on electronics and communications. Rachel, you said you were going to think about some question ideas.

Rachel   That's right. I've been looking at our subject of how household citizens in this country derive benefit from the digital environment. To start with, I thought we could ask about their perceptions of Internet speed.

Lance   Dial-up or broadband?

Rachel   <u>Broadband</u> I think, Lance. Not many people in this country have dial-up any more.

Abbie   I think that's a great start, Rachel. It's very topical at the moment. What about after that?

Rachel   Another important area is people's perceptions of affordability. This has a lot to do whether people have travelled to different countries and have seen the costs of services there and are therefore able to compare what they pay for here.

Lance   That's not necessarily true, Rachel. People can have perceptions of affordability without having to have travelled.

Abbie   That's true, Lance. I like the idea, Rachel, but let's keep the travel part out of it. If we include that, we could create too much <u>bias</u> within the answers, as people who don't travel wouldn't be able to answer.

Rachel   You're both right. I'll just make a note of that. Now, the next area I looked at was what people think about the possibility of changing subscriptions and switching between providers.

Martin   I thought it wasn't possible to just switch providers. Aren't people locked in with a contract?

Abbie   Yes, they are usually, but even within the contracts, there are ways of cancelling and changing provider.

Lance   There's also a lot of talk in the media about how many contracts demand three month <u>notice periods</u>. People often don't realise that and they're furious when they have to wait and pay for three further months.

Abbie   Yes, I know someone in that position. They're actually leaving the country and they have to continue paying their communications bill for two months, when they're not even in the country or living at the address that the contract deals with.

Martin　　　Well, we should get some good feedback and answers on that area.

Rachel　　　So, my next area is the transparency of <u>tariff information</u>. Again, this is a topical area in the communications industry.

Lance　　　That's right. There were some big stories in the media recently. The government has clamped down on companies not disclosing this.

Martin　　　I read a story last week about a family that sued their phone provider for not giving the proper information. The family won and it seems the government has finally woken up about this matter and will do something about it.

Abbie　　　Why is it so important?

Martin　　　It's because companies want people to choose the package that gives them the most <u>profit</u>. It doesn't matter to them that people don't get the deal that makes the most sense for them. Salespeople just give customers a limited number of options and customers can't find the full information anywhere else.

Abbie　　　That's awful. I can't believe they can get away with that nowadays.

Martin　　　I know. Fortunately, things are getting better though.

Rachel　　　So, the last area is about mobile phone usage.

Abbie　　　Will we just be looking at how often people use their mobile phones?

Rachel　　　Not so much that. We'll be more interested in how happy customers are with their signal reception.

Lance　　　That's a good topic too. I thought that we had good coverage in this country, but then I heard from some foreign student friends of mine that it's terrible here and that their countries are much better.

Rachel　　　That's right. We think it's OK here, as we're used to nothing different.

You now have some time to look at questions twenty-seven to thirty.

(20 second gap)

Now listen to the rest of the discussion and answer questions twenty-seven to thirty.

Lance　　　So, next we have to decide when and where to do our survey.

Abbie　　　I think the best thing would be to go after lectures on Wednesday morning. We'd get the afternoon shoppers and we'd get it all done before dinner.

Rachel   The problem with that is we'd only get people free on a weekday afternoon. There would be a lot of unemployed people and that would influence the results. On a Saturday afternoon, we'd get a lot more people and a better cross-section of society.

Abbie   I don't really want to lose my Saturday though.

Martin   Nor do I. I want to go to the football. Can't we do Friday afternoon? There'll be lots of people around off work early then.

Lance   Well, that would be better than Wednesday, but I think Rachel's right. Nobody wants to work at weekends, but if we want to do a good job with this survey, then we should make some sacrifices.

Abbie   OK.

Martin   Yes, I suppose the football can wait.

Lance   Now, are we sure that the town centre is the best place to conduct our survey? What do you think, Rachel?

Rachel   Well, it's the place where we'd find the most people. Also, we'd probably find the best cross-section of society there.

Martin   The trouble as I see it is that some people won't want to be stopped to answer our questions. You know what it's like.

Abbie   That's true, but that will be the same wherever we go. The other places where we'd find lots of people could be worse. In train and bus stations, people would be busy. I think Rachel's idea about the town centre is best.

Lance   What about in the central shopping mall?

Rachel   Again, maybe there would be too many of a certain type of people.

Martin   OK. I'm fine with Rachel's idea.

Lance   Me too. I'm happy.

Abbie   Finally, we need to analyse the information as fast as possible. Why don't you all come round to my place the next day and we can collate everything and do some statistical analysis. Can you make that, Lance?

Lance   I can't after three o'clock. I have to be with my family then. I could come before that or in the evening.

Abbie   How about you, Rachel?

Rachel   That should be no problem for me, as I'm free all day, so just let me know when. What about you, Martin?

Martin   It might be a problem for me, I'm afraid. I can come, but not in the evening. I've got tickets to the <u>cinema</u>.

Abbie   Let's meet at midday then. We should be able to get everything done in a couple of hours, so Lance can get away.

That is the end of section three. You will now have half a minute to check your answers.

(30 second gap)

Now turn to section four.

Section four. You will hear a lecture on geothermal energy. First you have some time to look at questions thirty-one to forty.

(50 second gap)

Now listen carefully and answer questions thirty-one to forty.

Hello everyone and welcome to this lecture on renewable energy resources. Today, we're going to look at geothermal energy and we'll look at the country of Iceland to see how this energy type has been exploited there.

Geothermal energy is the heat from the Earth. It's clean and sustainable. Resources of geothermal energy range from the shallow ground to hot water and hot rock found a few miles beneath the Earth's surface, and down even deeper to the layer of extremely high temperature magma. This layer of magma continually produces heat, mostly from the <u>decay</u> of naturally radioactive materials, such as uranium and potassium. The amount of heat within ten thousand meters of Earth's surface contains fifty thousand times more energy than all the oil and natural gas resources in the world.

Iceland is a pioneer in the use of geothermal energy for space heating. Generating electricity with geothermal energy has also increased significantly in recent years. Geothermal power facilities currently generate twenty-five per cent of the country's total electricity output. Last year, roughly eighty-four per cent of primary energy use in Iceland came from indigenous renewable resources, of which sixty-six per cent was geothermal. During the course of the twentieth century, Iceland went from what was one of Europe's lowest income countries, dependent upon peat and imported coal for its energy, to a country with a premier <u>standard of living</u>, where most energy is derived from renewable resources. The cheap source of energy created this change.

Iceland is a young country geologically. It lies astride one of the Earth's major fault lines, the Mid-Atlantic ridge. This is the boundary between the North American and Eurasian tectonic plates. The two plates are moving apart at a rate of about <u>two</u> centimetres per year. Iceland is an anomalous part of the ridge, where deep mantle material wells up and creates a hot spot of unusually great volcanic productivity. This makes Iceland one of the few places on Earth where one can see an active spreading ridge above sea level.

As a result of its location, Iceland is one of the most geologically active places on Earth, resulting in a large number of volcanoes and hot springs. Earthquakes are also frequent, but rarely cause serious damage. More than two hundred volcanoes are located within the active volcanic zone, stretching through the country from the southwest to the northeast, and at least thirty of them have erupted since the country was settled.

A lot of Iceland's geothermal energy comes from hot water or steam and these are found in two types of water temperature systems, high temperature fields and low temperature fields. High temperature fields are located within the active volcanic zones or marginal to them. They are mostly on high ground and the rocks are geologically very young and permeable. As a result of the topography and high bedrock permeability, the groundwater table in the high temperature areas is generally deep, and surface manifestations are largely steam vents.

The low temperature fields are all located outside the volcanic zone passing through Iceland. The largest examples of these systems are located in southwest Iceland, on the flanks of the western volcanic zone, but smaller systems can be found throughout the country. On the surface, low temperature activity is manifested in hot or boiling springs, although no surface indications are observed on top of some such systems. Flow rates range from almost zero to a maximum of one hundred and eighty litres per second from a single spring. Scientists believe these low temperature fields are transient, lasting some thousands of years.

There are three ways to create electricity with geothermal energy. Hydrothermal, using hot water, geopressurised, using a hydraulic turbine, and petrothermal, using superheated dry rock to create steam when water is pumped into it. In Iceland, generating electricity with geothermal energy has increased significantly in recent years and as a result of a rapid expansion in Iceland's energy intensive industry, the demand for electricity has increased considerably. One of the most common electricity generation methods in Iceland is with a geothermal plant, which brings heat up to the surface, where it is brought into contact with water. This creates high pressure steam, which is then piped to drive turbines. The pipes and turbines must be extremely strong in order to stop the corrosive steam from bursting out and causing a danger to workers. The turbines in turn create the electromagnetic field within a generator that creates electricity. The electricity generated is then transferred out to a local substation, before being directed to its place of end use. Back at the geothermal plant, the steam that has been through the turbines is piped away. The steam is then allowed to condense in a cooling tower. Warm air and vapour is released into the air and the left-over hot water is piped away for a variety of other direct heat uses, such as house heating, agriculture, fish farms and industry.

That is the end of section four. You will now have half a minute to check your answers.

(30 second gap)

That is the end of listening test eleven. In the IELTS test you would now have ten minutes to transfer your answers to the listening answer sheet.

LISTENING TEST 12 TRANSCRIPT

This recording is copyright.

IELTS-Blog.com listening practice tests. Test twelve. In the IELTS test you hear some recordings and you have to answer questions on them. You have time to read the instructions and questions and check your work. All recordings are played only once. The test is in four sections. Now turn to section one.

Section one. You will hear a conversation between a man and a woman as they discuss a hiking holiday in Scotland.

First you have some time to look at questions one to five.

(20 second gap)

You will see that there is an example. This time only, the conversation relating to this will be played first.

Graham	So, Sophie. Are you ready to talk about our holiday in Scotland?
Sophie	Oh yes. I'm looking forward to getting things finalised.
Graham	So, we start our holiday in Oban, then we go to Skye and after that to Lewis.
Sophie	That's right.

So, Oban is the correct answer.

Now the full test will begin. You should answer the questions as you listen, as the recording is not played twice. Listen carefully to the conversation and answer questions one to five.

Graham	So, Sophie. Are you ready to talk about our holiday in Scotland?
Sophie	Oh yes. I'm looking forward to getting things finalised.
Graham	So, we start our holiday in <u>Oban</u>, then we go to Skye and after that to Lewis.
Sophie	That's right.
Graham	Now, <u>we're staying in Oban for five nights from the eighth of July</u> until the thirteenth. Is that right?
Sophie	I thought we were one day earlier. Let's have a look. No, you're right. It's from the eighth. It's my grandmother's birthday on the seventh and I got mixed up.
Graham	Good, that's settled then. It wouldn't have been a good start if we got the dates wrong!
Sophie	No. I remember that I wanted to be at home for grandma's birthday and that we could leave the next day.
Graham	So, the next thing should be how we're going to get to Oban.
Sophie	Well, as I see it, we have the choice of driving up, the train or the bus.

Graham   Yes. Driving up wouldn't be the cheapest, but it would be the fastest. However, as we're going on a hiking holiday, we won't need the car at all after we've arrived.

Sophie   And as we're taking the ferry to Lewis, it'll be cheaper not to have the car and travel as foot passengers.

Graham   The bus would be convenient then, as it takes us straight to Oban with only one change.

Sophie   The train does as well.

Graham   That's true, though I checked and if we book the bus in advance, the train will be twice as expensive.

Sophie   Well, let's go for the cheapest option then. The bus won't be that much longer. Are you OK with that?

Graham   Yes, that's fine. We can use the money we save on spoiling ourselves when we're there!

Sophie   So, what's next?

Graham   We have to decide on where we're going to stay.

Sophie   Yes. Now, you know I said I'd check some places out?

Graham   Yes. You said that you would order some magazines.

Sophie   Well, I had a look at some places online, but I didn't have much time and I didn't manage to do anything else.

Graham   That's OK. Don't worry. I know that you were really busy.

Sophie   Yes. I had good intentions, but they didn't work out.

Graham   So, now we have to decide what kind of place we want to stay in. The choice is really a hostel, a guest house or a hotel.

Sophie   I'm tired of staying in cheap hostels and I've had a look at the guest houses and there's not a great selection.

Graham   I agree. So, we'll go for a hotel then.

Sophie   Yes. We can use the money we saved on the travel!

Graham   OK. Now, do you want to have breakfast and dinner at the hotel?

Sophie   I'd say so. It would be very convenient. Breakfast would be waiting for us every morning and in the evenings we'd be tired after our hiking and not too keen to go out.

Graham   That's true, but Oban has great places to eat and I think we should make the effort to get out in the evenings and try some places. Oban's small and nothing will be too far away.

Sophie   OK. I'll go along with that. I still think breakfast would be better at the hotel though.

Graham   Yes, I agree with that.

Page 160

Before the conversation continues, you have some time to look at questions six to ten.

(20 second gap)

Now listen carefully and answer questions six to ten.

Sophie   So, have you researched any hiking routes when we get to Oban?

Graham   Yes, I've looked at a few. My favourite one is a coastal route that goes from Oban to a small town called Dunbeg.

Sophie   Tell me about it.

Graham   It's a nice easy one to start with. This is because we stick to the coast, so there are no <u>hills</u> to deal with. We'd start after breakfast and head north and move up and hug the coast. The hike will take about three and a half hours and the end point is Dunbeg, which is inland a little.

Sophie   Are there any good things to see?

Graham   Yes. There are the views of the sea and of course the island of Kerrera, across from Oban. Soon we'll pass Saint Columba's cathedral and near the end of the walk, there's a spectacular ruined castle next to the sea. At the end, we can get a <u>bus</u> back from Dunbeg.

Sophie   How long does the bus take?

Graham   Only about a quarter of an hour. We can walk back the way we came or walk back along the road, but I thought it would be nice to have lunch in Dunbeg and then get back to Oban quickly and spend the afternoon looking around the town.

Sophie   That all sounds fine. Have you found any other hikes?

Graham   You know I mentioned the island of Kerrera earlier?

Sophie   Yes.

Graham   Well, for the second day's hike we can get a ferry across to the island from Oban and there are a number of routes there. The easiest and most popular route is the southern one and again we'll get to see a castle.

Sophie   Is it a demanding route?

Graham   Not at all. The hike is approximately <u>five</u> miles in total and I think it will take us at least three hours for it. The island is mostly flat and the path is well-tended. It shouldn't stretch us very much.

Sophie   I expect there'll be a lot of sea views again being an island. I really like that.

Graham   Actually not as much as you'd think, as we'll be going inland a lot.

Sophie   We'll have seen a lot of the sea the day before, so that's fine.

Graham   That's what I thought.

Sophie   Good. I'll be quite unfit and I want to break into things slowly. We can go for harder hikes later in the holiday.

Page 161

Graham   Exactly. So, to make this hike into a day trip, we can look around the castle, as it was restored a few years ago. We can also take a picnic and relax next to a good view.

Sophie   Well, that's the first two days then. Now, the first hike should be easy to find our way, as we're just following the coastline, but the second could be harder if we're going inland.

Graham   Yes, I thought about that. I went onto the island's website and we can buy a map on the ferry while we're crossing over.

Sophie   Oh good. Well done. You seem to have done some good research.

Graham   Thanks. I'm quite excited about our trip.

That is the end of section one. You will now have half a minute to check your answers.

(30 second gap)

Now turn to section two.

Section two. You will hear a woman telling a group information about a museum tour. First you have some time to look at questions eleven to fifteen.

(20 second gap)

Now listen carefully to the information talk and answer questions eleven to fifteen.

Good afternoon everyone and welcome to this tour of the Weyport museum. My name is Victoria and I'll be showing you round today. This will be a two-hour tour and I'll show you all the key exhibits that we possess. Naturally, we won't be able to look at everything, but the museum will remain open for three hours after the tour ends, so you'll be able to see anything you missed then.

The building that the museum stands in today has been here since the late nineteenth century. It was built by the local Weyport town council and owned by them until ten years ago, although the use of the building changed several times during their ownership. Ten years ago, the town council allowed the building to be bought by a group of enthusiasts that had been canvassing for a larger and better-equipped town museum for quite a few years. They had gained cash from a variety of fund raising activities that were supported by the general public. The existing small museum was happy to merge with the new one and allow the new one to take all the exhibits and the previous museum director continued in his post at the new museum. The new museum's purchase was also assisted financially by the local engineering company, Ryland Limited, whose managing director is a great patron of the arts. At first, the local council wasn't too keen on letting go of the building, but the central arts council in London liked the idea of the new museum and applied some administrative pressure. The local council agreed and the sale went through fairly quickly.

As I said, the history of the building was varied. It started off as an office administration centre for the local council. Unfortunately, there was a fire in nineteen twenty and after that, the building lay unused for a number of years. There was a lack of funds for renovation, in spite of the insurance pay out. From nineteen thirty, the building was made safe and used as a storage facility for old files and other records belonging to the town council. The army tried to gain control of the building to use as a recruitment centre during World War Two, but the building was deemed too unsafe for the projected numbers of people. After the war, the building continued its pre-war use until the nineteen sixties, when <u>the council used the building for its local education department.</u> The building remained like this until it was sold for the new museum. The education department moved to the new council offices on the edge of town and is found next to the housing department.

You now have some time to look at questions sixteen to twenty.

(20 second gap)

Now listen to the rest of the information talk and answer questions sixteen to twenty.

So, we'll begin the tour on the ground floor. Right now, we're in the reception hall where you all bought your tickets. We've just come in through the main doors with the ticket office opposite. <u>We'll start by going in through the door on the right. If you go left, you'll find the museum's bathrooms.</u> You'll need to come back here if you want to use them.

<u>So, in this first room on the right, we'll find our collections of paintings.</u> We have mostly pictures by local painters. No one is particularly famous, but the quality is very high and we get visitors from all over the country. <u>We continue the tour into the next two rooms, where we will find very unusual exhibitions. This town is famous for its factories that manufacture clocks and silverware. The clock collection from the local factories comes first and then the following room focuses on silverware. In the corner of the silverware room, there is a room where you can see a film</u> that explains the history of both our town's famous industries.

Moving round into the next room, we'll find displays from the town's Iron Age history. There are examples of a variety of things that have been discovered in and around the town. We have old pots, jewelry, weapons, examples of surviving architecture and plenty of photographs of local archaeological sites. The next room houses the museum's café, where you can get hot or cold drinks and some snacks to eat. <u>Finally, the last room on the ground floor holds our collection of antique children's toys.</u> It's amazing to see the range of things that were manufactured and this room is always a favourite with visitors. After we've finished there, we'll move up the stairs to the first floor, where we'll continue.

That is the end of section two. You will now have half a minute to check your answers.

(30 second gap)

Now turn to section three.

Section three. You will hear three students discussing a field trip. First you have some time to look at questions twenty-one to twenty-five.

(20 second gap)

Now listen carefully and answer questions twenty-one to twenty-five.

Ellie	Hi Alan.
Alan	Hi Ellie. Hi Janet. How are you both today?
Janet	Hi Alan. We're both good. Are you ready to discuss our field trip?
Alan	Sure. That's why I'm here.

Ellie   Good. Let's get started. We're going to go on a trip down the coast to look at cliff formations. We know the date we're going, so <u>the first thing is that we need to decide how to get there.</u>

Alan   Yes. The options are hiring a car for the day or getting the bus. The car will be more flexible, but the bus will be cheaper.

Janet   I'll go down to the bus station this afternoon and check prices and times and then I'll go to that local car hire company next to the supermarket and get a quote.

Ellie   Good. Now, <u>we have the general area where we want to go, but we need to narrow down our survey area exactly.</u>

Alan   I've had a look at the map. The best area would be from Durham Rocks to Long Beach.

Janet   Why there?

Alan   First of all, there's a car park and bus stop next to the Durham Rocks and there are also paths at the top of the cliff and at its foot at low tide along the beach. We'll get good access for our survey.

Ellie   Well done, Alan. <u>How long do you think the survey will take?</u>

Alan   <u>I reckon about five hours to do a good job. We won't need to stay overnight like some of the other groups. That's good, as there are no hostels or anything where we're going.</u>

Janet   What things do we need to take with us?

Ellie   The usual survey stuff. <u>Maps, compasses, a level kit and a rangefinder.</u>

Janet   <u>Can we get all that?</u>

Ellie   <u>The department has it all and we can book it out as long as no one's got there first. I'll do that this afternoon when I go in for our lecture.</u>

Alan   Thanks, Ellie.

Janet   <u>Is there any food available where we're going? We'll be there for quite some time and if things take longer than expected, we'll get hungry.</u>

Alan   <u>I'll check that out online. My laptop's at home right now, but I'll need to get it before my lecture. I'll do it when I get home. If there's nowhere to eat, I'll make some sandwiches and bring some water or something.</u> I'll let you know at the lecture.

Ellie   Well, that's the organisation part done for the time being. Let's just hope it doesn't rain! I don't fancy spending five hours under an umbrella.

You now have some time to look at questions twenty-six to thirty.

(20 second gap)

Now listen to the rest of the discussion and answer questions twenty-six to thirty.

Janet　　　　So, why are we going to that area of the coast anyway? There are plenty of cliffs much closer to us.

Alan　　　　It's all to do with the erosion of the cliffs in that area. There are some really classic examples there. Do you remember that lecture we had on coastal erosion?

Janet　　　　I missed that lecture, as I was sick.

Ellie　　　　I'll explain. The cliffs in that area mostly consist of <u>sand</u> and clay with very little rock. This makes them very susceptible to erosion.

Janet　　　　Do all coastlines suffer from erosion?

Alan　　　　It depends. Both exposed and sheltered coasts can suffer from it. The coast has to receive the power of the sea in a certain direction and force. Currents, winds and tides also play a key role.

Ellie　　　　Where we're going, the sea comes right up to the cliffs at <u>high tide</u>. The waves can then batter the soft lower parts of the cliffs. At low tide, we can walk in front of the cliffs for our survey.

Janet　　　　Does that make it dangerous to walk at the top of the cliffs?

Alan　　　　It can be. Fortunately, the area where we're going has paths set well back and there are fences to keep people away from edges that might be dangerous. We won't need to go close to the edges of the cliffs, anyway.

Janet　　　　So, what happens when the waves hit the lower parts of the cliffs?

Ellie　　　　It's simple really. The cliff is worn away and an <u>undercut</u> is made. The deeper this becomes, the more unstable the cliff above becomes. When the weight above becomes too much, then the cliff collapses.

Alan　　　　This of course can cause problems if there is anything significant on top of the cliffs.

Janet　　　　It sounds like it's dangerous to be under the cliffs as well.

Alan　　　　Yes, it is. <u>The coastguard</u> is responsible for keeping a close eye on the cliffs though and you can check on the dangerous areas on their website. There are lots of signs in dangerous areas, too.

Janet　　　　Before we go, we'd better check on that and the tides as well, as they can come in quickly.

Alan　　　　I intend to.

Ellie　　　　Don't worry, Janet. We won't go into any danger areas.

Janet　　　　Should we take flares in case we get into any problems?

Alan　　　　No, I don't think that's necessary. We'll all just take <u>our mobile phones</u> with us. If we do run into any trouble, we can then call the authorities. It really won't be a problem, Janet. If I thought we'd be in any danger, I'd take an inflatable boat with us or not go at all!

That is the end of section three. You will now have half a minute to check your answers.

(30 second gap)

Now turn to section four.

Section four. You will hear a lecture on the Wechsler-Belleview Intelligence Scale. First you have some time to look at questions thirty-one to forty.

(50 second gap)

Now listen carefully and answer questions thirty-one to forty.

Good morning everyone and welcome to this psychology lecture. Today, we are going to look at one of the most common tests that is used to assess intelligence. Many tests have been created for this purpose, but we are focusing this morning on the Wechsler-Belleview Intelligence Scale.

Doctor David Wechsler, a clinical psychologist at New York's Belleview hospital, believed that intelligence is a global construct, reflecting a variety of measurable skills and should be considered in the setting of the <u>overall personality</u>. Dissatisfied with the intelligence tests in vogue when he started practising, Wechsler created intelligence scales that included many novel concepts and breakthroughs to the intelligence testing movement. He did away with the quotient scores of older intelligence tests, or the Q in IQ. Instead, he assigned an arbitrary value of a hundred to the <u>mean intelligence</u> and added or subtracted fifteen points for each standard deviation above or below the subject's mean.

The theoretical basis for the Wechsler-Belleview Intelligence Scale and the other Wechlser scales came from this belief of Wechsler's that intelligence is a complex ability involving a variety of skills. Because intelligence is multifaceted, Wechsler believed a test measuring intelligence must reflect this multitude of skills. Wechsler divided the concept of intelligence into two principal areas: <u>verbal</u> and performance, and further subdivided and tested each area with a different subtest.

Wechsler's full scale test is broken down into fourteen sub-tests, comprising the verbal scale, seven verbal sub-tests, the performance scale and seven performance sub-tests. Wechsler's tests provide three scores: a verbal IQ score, a performance IQ score, and a composite IQ score based on the combined scores. Verbal subtests aim to test general cultural information, abstract comprehension, arithmetic, verbal reasoning, vocabulary, concentration, and memory. Performance subtests include visual perception, visual-motor coordination, spatial perception, abstract problem solving, sequential reasoning, perception speed, and visual analysis. These conceptualisations continue to be reflected in the Wechsler scales of the twenty-first century and the Wechsler-Belleview Intelligence Scale continues to remain the most commonly administered <u>psychological test</u> in existence.

The Wechsler Adult Intelligence Scale is appropriate throughout adulthood. For testing children aged seven to sixteen, the Wechsler Intelligence Scale for Children is used, while the Wechsler Preschool and Primary Scale of Intelligence is used for testing children aged two and a half to seven. Both tests can be completed without a <u>literacy</u> requirement in their subjects.

Although the Wechsler-Belleview Intelligence Scale is regarded as extremely useful and accurate, it does have some limitations. As long as test administrators realise this, the test can be used very reliably for its designed purposes. The limitations are not serious. It is not considered for measuring extremes of intelligence, which are indicated by IQ scores below forty and above one hundred and sixty. Wechsler himself was even more conservative, stressing that his scales were not appropriate for people with an IQ below seventy or above one hundred and thirty. Also, when administering the Wechsler Adult Intelligence Scale to people at <u>extreme ends</u> of the age range, such as below twenty years of age or above seventy, caution should be used for <u>the interpretation</u> of scores.

Besides being used as an intelligence assessment, one other use of the Wechsler-Belleview Intelligence Scale is that it can be used for neuropsychological evaluation, as large differences in answers testing verbal and non-verbal intelligence may be a sign of specific sorts of <u>brain damage</u>. Intelligence scores reported by the Wechsler-Belleview Intelligence Scale can also be used as part of the diagnostic criteria for learning disabilities and attention deficit hyperactivity disorder. However, the consensus of professionals in the field is that the Wechsler-Belleview Intelligence Scale is best used as a tool to evaluate intelligence and not to diagnose ADHD or learning disabled children. Nevertheless, many clinicians use it to compare a child's cognitive development to his or her actual social or <u>school</u> capabilities. Using discrepancies in the scale and other sources of data, the Wechsler-Belleview Intelligence Scale can contribute information concerning a child's psychological well-being.

So, to conclude the first part of this lecture, the Wechsler-Belleview Intelligence Scale is regularly used by researchers in many areas of psychology as a measure of intelligence and it is considered to be a valid and reliable measure of general intelligence. It is so well regarded that other intelligence tests are often compared to it when undergoing <u>reliability</u> and validity studies.

That is the end of section four. You will now have half a minute to check your answers.

(30 second gap)

That is the end of listening test twelve. In the IELTS test you would now have ten minutes to transfer your answers to the listening answer sheet.

LISTENING TEST 13 TRANSCRIPT

This recording is copyright.

IELTS-Blog.com listening practice tests. Test thirteen. In the IELTS test you hear some recordings and you have to answer questions on them. You have time to read the instructions and questions and check your work. All recordings are played only once. The test is in four sections. Now turn to section one.

Section one. You will hear a conversation between a man and a woman discussing the enrollment of the man's child at a nursery.

First you have some time to look at questions one to five.

(20 second gap)

You will see that there is an example. This time only, the conversation relating to this will be played first.

Laura	Good morning. My name's Laura. Welcome to Happies Nursery. How can I help you today?
Luke with you.	Good morning. My wife and I were hoping that we might be able to enrol our daughter
Laura	We do have space, so that should be fine. What's the age of your daughter?
Luke	She's two.

So, two is the correct answer.

Now the full test will begin. You should answer the questions as you listen, as the recording is not played twice. Listen carefully to the conversation and answer questions one to five.

Laura	Good morning. My name's Laura. Welcome to Happies Nursery. How can I help you today?
Luke with you.	Good morning. My wife and I were hoping that we might be able to enrol our daughter
Laura	We do have space, so that should be fine. What's the age of your daughter?
Luke	She's two.
Laura	OK. Now, I need to take some details first.
Luke	Of course.
Laura	To begin with, I need your and your wife's names.
Luke	My name is Luke Beckett and my wife's name is Gloria Beckett.
Laura	Would you spell Beckett for me, please?
Luke	It's B - E - C - K - E - T - T.

Page 168

Laura   And Gloria?

Luke   G - L - O - R - I - A.

Laura   Thank you. And can I assume that you both live together at the same address?

Luke   Yes, we do.

Laura   Can I have the full address?

Luke   It's forty Castle Crescent. Backley.

Laura   And the post code?

Luke   It's BA three seven TR.

Laura   Thank you. Now, can I take some telephone numbers for you and your wife?

Luke   Of course. Our home number is oh one five three eight, eight five three, two eight five.

Laura   Thank you. And do you have mobile numbers?

Luke   Yes. Mine is oh seven seven seven oh, seven two eight four seven three and my wife's is oh seven seven four three, eight one two, four five one.

Laura   Could you say your wife's again, please?

Luke   Of course. It's oh seven seven four three, eight one two, four five one.

Laura   Thanks. I've got all that down. Could I also have work numbers for you both?

Luke   My office number is oh one five three eight, nine two six, four seven seven and my wife's work number is oh one five three eight, five nine six, eight two one.

Laura   Thanks. Now, I'll talk about our fee structure a little later, but how would you like to pay
our fees?

Luke   We'll pay by bank transfer when we get the invoice.

Laura   That's fine. Thank you. So, your daughter. What's her name?

Luke   It's Gertrude Beckett. She has no middle name.

Laura   Good. She's two years old. I know that. Does she have any allergies that you know of?

Luke   The only one we know of is that she's allergic to cats.

Laura   OK. I've made a note of that. It won't be a problem. There are no animals in our nursery and none of our teachers has a pet.

Luke   Good. That's very reassuring.

Before the conversation continues, you have some time to look at questions six to ten.

(20 second gap)

Now listen carefully and answer questions six to ten.

Laura   Now, I suppose you know quite a lot about us already, as you've chosen us to look after your daughter.

Luke   That's right. We have friends who have their children here.

Laura   That's good. I'd still like to talk about our systems here a little bit though.

Luke   Oh yes. That's fine.

Laura   So, we start doing activities at <u>eight thirty</u> a.m., but parents can drop off their children at any time after six thirty. From six thirty, we always have a team of carers here who will supervise your child whilst she plays with the others and they will clean and change her when necessary. You don't need to bring anything in that regard, as we will have all that is necessary here.

Luke   Do we need to bring anything else for Gertrude?

Laura   Just a sweater for going outside and a couple of <u>changes of clothing</u> in case she gets dirty. Keep it in a good quality bag and have it clearly marked as Gertrude's.

Luke   OK. What, what happens if Gertrude's sick?

Laura   We will of course call you and your wife straight away if she's sick. You'll need to pick her up as soon as you can when that happens, as we don't want other children to catch illnesses. In the unlikely event of anything really serious, we're just a mile away from the County Hospital. Also, we always have a <u>nurse</u> on duty who specialises in children, so your child will always have good supervision in terms of health.

Luke   Good. Thank you.

Laura   The end of day-time activities is at four o'clock, though you can pick Gertrude up earlier if you wish. Also, we offer supervision until six thirty for people who work late. We ask that you do not arrive later than that to pick up your child, as our staff will want to get home to their families. If you're unavoidably detained, please call our number, which is in our <u>information pack</u> here.

Luke   That shouldn't be a problem for us, as we both finish work at around four o'clock.

Laura   Good. Finally, I'd like to tell you about a new service that we're running. It will cost extra outside our usual fee structure, but it's proving to be incredibly popular. We now offer supervision at the <u>weekends</u>, so that parents can be free to shop, travel a little or do other necessary things that would be awkward with a young child.

Luke   I don't think we'd need that often, as we wouldn't like to leave Gertrude then as we see her so little during the week. It would be very useful for unexpected things and emergencies though.

Laura   Well, let's move on to the fee structure.

That is the end of section one. You will now have half a minute to check your answers.

(30 second gap)

Now turn to section two.

Page 170

Section two. You will hear a man giving some people information about an old age care centre. First you have some time to look at questions eleven to fifteen.

(20 second gap)

Now listen carefully to the information talk and answer questions eleven to fifteen.

Good morning everyone and welcome to this open day at the Green Trees Old Age Centre. My name is Charlie and I would like to tell you a little about us today. I have met some of you already and I know that some of you are thinking of coming to stay here yourselves and some of you are here to see it we will suit a friend or relative of yours.

So, we offer skilled elderly care for up to <u>sixty</u> residents. We have places for both men and women, with men being accommodated on the first floor and women on the second floor. We have three lifts that service all the floors for those who find stairs challenging. All our rooms are single and therefore we are not suited to looking after <u>married couples</u> together. All our rooms are en suite and are cleaned daily. Some types of pet are allowed, but this has to be discussed with the manager. The manager will decide on a case-by-case basis.

The common areas are exceptionally luxurious. We have lounges, television rooms and a games room, which are open to all residents. Our dining room is as well-appointed as the rest of our facilities and our food is exceptional. Breakfast, lunch and dinner are served of course every day and <u>specialised diets</u>, for example for diabetics, can be catered for after consultation. If residents get hungry between meals, there is coffee and tea available mid-morning with snacks, and afternoon tea is served every day with sandwiches and cakes. In good weather in the summer, afternoon tea is served outside on the lawn.

One important part of any old age centre is our facilities for nursing. Older people need a special type of care the older they get and this must be combined with opportunities to retain the chances for being <u>independent</u> as much as is practical. Green Trees has full-time nurses on duty twenty-four hours a day. These nurses have specialised in old age care and are all greatly experienced in this field. We also have access to extra specialised carers when the need arises. In addition to this, we have a local GP who visits twice a week. This GP is also able to visit at other times when necessary, including at night time.

Green Trees is a fee-charging establishment. I don't want to tell you all about our fees here, but all the details are available on our leaflets by the door and also on the <u>website</u>. The fees advertised are our current ones, but be aware that fees change every six months, depending on our own costs.

You now have some time to look at questions sixteen to twenty.

(20 second gap)

Now listen to the rest of the information talk and answer questions sixteen to twenty.

Green Trees also has a variety of activities for our residents, both inside and outside our premises. Our activities provide our residents opportunities to have fun, exercise their brains and bodies, and meet new friends.

Twice weekly, we have sessions in our games room. This includes playing cards, bingo, board games, quizzes and lots of other activities. At Green Trees, we know it's important to meet different people and so residents are always allowed to invite a <u>guest</u> to these evenings. In this way, everyone gets to meet new people and develop new friendships. We also have regular puzzle sessions at different times of the day, with crosswords, sudoku and other stimulating and fun activities. One exciting and new venture that we're doing right now is getting residents to tell their life stories. Sometimes it's not so easy to recall everything, but the attempt often brings back things previously forgotten. We also encourage the recollections to be recorded or written down, which is great for younger relatives, who find out things that they never would do otherwise. All these activities lead to fitness in the <u>brain</u> for seniors and this has become an important part of lifelong well-being.

It's equally important to get out of Green Trees from time to time. We run regular visits to the theatre, ballet, opera, cinema, local markets and to places of local interest. We only organise <u>one-day</u> trips, in case our residents get too tired. Family members can of course take residents out for overnight trips or longer whenever they want. We ask, of course, to be kept informed of any time spent away, so we can organise our food and care schedules accordingly.

One very popular activity in Green Trees is gardening. We have extended gardens and when the weather is appropriate, residents can change their clothes and go outside and get dirty! Gardening can be a very fulfilling activity for the elderly. Tending plants can overcome feelings of <u>isolation</u> by giving individuals the opportunity to play a more active part in the world around them. Being responsible for the care of plants can also help residents feel more in control. The problem for a lot of elderly people is that manual work in the garden can cause serious aches and pains, whilst also worsening existing problems. We will give you training and the <u>special tools</u> that will help you stay safe and healthy. Our two gardeners will also be there to supervise and give advice and I'm afraid residents also have to follow their orders about what is planted and where!

That is the end of section two. You will now have half a minute to check your answers.

(30 second gap)

Now turn to section three.

Section three. You will hear four students discussing their engineering work placements. First you have some time to look at questions twenty-one to twenty-five.

(20 second gap)

Now listen carefully and answer questions twenty-one to twenty-five.

Ross	Hi Tanya.
Tanya	Hi Ross, hi Derek.
Derek	Hi Tanya. Have you seen Lily?
Tanya	Yes, she's just behind me. Here she is.
Lily	Hi everyone.
Derek	Hi Lily. You know Ross, don't you?
Lily	Yes, I do. Hi Ross.
Ross	Hi Lily. So, Lily, do you know what you're doing for your engineering work placement?

Lily　　　　Well, you know I applied for something in aviation engineering?

Ross　　　　Yes.

Lily　　　　Unfortunately, my application for that was turned down, so I also applied for a practical job, working on bridge construction in Brisbane.

Tanya　　　Was that successful?

Lily　　　　No. They called and said someone else had taken the job, so I applied for a job helping in an engineering office in town.

Derek　　　So, that's what you're doing?

Lily　　　　They offered me and I was about to accept when the bridge people called and said the person who'd accepted had dropped out, so I've ended up with that.

Ross　　　　Well done. You'll learn a lot with that.

Tanya　　　Yes, and it'll look great on your CV.

Lily　　　　I'm sure it will. It's not aviation, but it'll still be very interesting. What about you, Ross?

Ross　　　　Oh, I didn't have too much trouble. Fortunately my father has an engineering firm, so he's taken me on.

Tanya　　　That should be great fun.

Ross　　　　It might be, but you don't know my Dad. He'll work me to death. It might've been better just to have done some road surveying for the local government. That would've been boring, but at least nine to five.

Derek　　　I thought that you'd applied for work on an oil rig off Borneo.

Ross　　　　I wanted to do that, but they said I didn't have the breadth of knowledge for working there. And Derek, what about your plans?

Derek　　　I had a placement working out in the Antarctic, but I had to turn it down.

Tanya　　　Oh no. Why?

Derek　　　I was worried about the extreme cold, but they said that I'd be OK with that. My Dad's a doctor in a hospital and he said that the months I was there would present no problems. However, my old trouble with blood circulation was noticed by the company supervisor working there and she said it was too big a risk being so far from a hospital, in case this came back.

Tanya　　　That's a shame.

Derek　　　Yes, it is, but I've got a good placement in Brisbane's department of roads. That fits in with what I want to do when I graduate, so things worked out well in the end.

Lily　　　　So, that leaves you, Tanya.

Tanya　　　I had three offers in the end.

Ross   Good for you. What were they?

Tanya   My tutor recommended working in a ship building yard, as he's got some contacts there. He said I'd get a really constructive job there. The second was in gas drilling, as my cousin works in that and he said he'd sort me out with something with him where I'd learn a lot. The last was for the city engineering department. My boyfriend works there and he wants me to be close.

Derek   Which did you choose?

Tanya   Well, I've always been interested in geology and the search for underground wealth, so I chose the one searching for gas. That's the field I'd like to work in after graduation, although I'll find myself far away from any civilisation for most of my time. This one is right out in the desert.

Lily   By the way, how do we notify our department about our choices? Do we just call them or tell our tutors?

Ross   There's an online form that needs to be printed out and filled in. I don't think you can send it as an attachment.

Tanya   Ross is right. It needs to be signed by your tutor and they need an original for their copy, so it needs to be given in face to face.

Derek   You'd think that nowadays they'd accept a scan of a signed document that was sent by email. I mean it's valid legally.

Lily   You know our professors. Some of them don't even know how to open their email!

You now have some time to look at questions twenty-six to thirty.

(20 second gap)

Now listen to the rest of the discussion and answer questions twenty-six to thirty.

Derek   So, Tanya, working in the desert! That'll be a bit scary, won't it?

Tanya   I expect when I go at the start, it'll be a bit frightening, but I've been told that you get used to it very quickly.

Ross   So, you're drilling for gas?

Tanya   That's right.

Lily   That sounds interesting. We haven't studied many things like that though.

Tanya   I know, so I've been studying it myself for a couple of months. The gas drilling station is a fairly standard assembly. The well head is where the hole to the gas reservoir starts and it's above ground, next to a monitoring facility. That's where I'll be most of the time. The drill has to pass first through the normal earth until it hits a shale rock layer at around forty metres. After that, it passes through some cap rock and finally some storage rock. Then it hits the gas reservoir.

Ross   Is it a long process?

Page 174

Tanya   Quite long. The shale rock is easy to pass through, but the other layers are very hard and thick.

Derek   So, once the drill hits the gas reservoir, it's just a matter of monitoring.

Tanya   No. There's a constant need for working out how much gas is left and where the best place is to get it from. This means other holes may need to be drilled and that's what I'll be doing. We have secondary holes at different depths to the side of the primary drill hole and underground sensors at the bottom send up information to the monitoring facility. This data then needs to be analysed.

Ross   It'll be a fantastic thing to do, Tanya. And it'll be great experience. If you want to work in that field later, it'll really help you find a job.

Lily   It'll be quite a lot of pressure on you also. You'll be in the desert with a few colleagues, making drilling decisions that will cost a lot of money.

Tanya   Not quite. We'll be analysing the data, but we'll be connected by satellite to the head offices and it'll be the people there who make the decisions of whether to drill or not.

Lily   Oh good. That'll take the stress away. I'd hate to think what would happen if I had to make all the decisions out there.

Tanya   I don't think they'd let me do all the decision by myself in any situation. Anyway, it's not as if I'll be on my own out there!

Derek   Don't you think you'll go crazy being stuck out there in the desert? Our placements are for six months and after six months in the desert, I'd be feeling very strange.

Tanya   It won't be that bad. The teams that work out there are on four-week rotations. Everyone then gets a week off and then they go to a different station. My situation will be different. After my four-week rotations, I'll be taken back to the city for four weeks and then I'll just do nine to five on weekdays at the head offices until I return to my drilling station. It's a good mixture. Back in the head offices, I'll be able to see what they do with the data that we collect out in the desert.

Ross   Well, that all sounds very exciting.

That is the end of section three. You will now have half a minute to check your answers.

(30 second gap)

Now turn to section four.

Section four. You will hear a lecture on hypnosis, hypnotism and hypnotherapy. First you have some time to look at questions thirty-one to forty.

(50 second gap)

Now listen carefully and answer questions thirty-one to forty.

Hello everyone. Today in our psychology lecture, we're going to look at hypnosis, hypnotism and hypnotherapy.

First of all, let's look at some definitions. Hypnosis is an inferred psychophysiological state characterised by greater possibilities for <u>influence</u>, and is thought to be an altered state of consciousness. Hypnotism is the study and use of suggestion with the presence of hypnosis, while hypnotherapy, or clinical hypnosis, as it's sometimes referred to, is a form of therapy in which the use of hypnotism constitutes the core of the treatment. Simply speaking, hypnosis is an altered state of consciousness. Hypnotherapy, therefore, is the use of an altered state of consciousness, or trance, for a therapeutic endpoint. This means that people are not treated with hypnosis, but are treated in hypnosis.

All hypnotic states are characterised by a tremendously pleasant state of calm, which individuals allow themselves to enter, so that desired and beneficial suggestions may be given directly to the part of the mind known as the <u>subconscious</u>. Under hypnosis, the conscious and rational part of the brain is temporarily avoided, making the subconscious part, which influences mental and physical functions, receptive to therapy. During the trance state, there is heightened <u>concentration</u> for the specific purpose of maximising potential, changing limiting beliefs and behaviours and gaining insight and wisdom.

Although hypnosis may be light, medium or deep, a medium trance is usually used, during which breathing and the heartbeat slow and the brain produces alpha waves. Normal levels of consciousness, such as sleeping, dreaming or being awake, can be detected in the wave patterns produced by the brain. The state of hypnosis differs from all three. In alpha states, the body gradually achieves a particular <u>relaxation</u>. Hypnosis, meditation, day dreaming, being absorbed in a book or music or television, driving and arriving at your destination without recalling all the usual hallmarks are good examples of alpha states.

It is still not well known how hypnosis influences the brain. One popular theory is that it affects the mechanisms of attention, which occurs in one area of the brain called the ascending reticular formation, located in the brain stem. This area, which has many functions related to sleep, alertness and the sensorial perception, continuously bombards the rest of the brain with stimuli coming from the <u>sense organs</u>. The inhibition of the ascending reticular formation leads to states of extreme calm.

So, how does hypnotherapy work? The subconscious mind is the source of many of our problems and self images and our beliefs, habits and behaviours are stored there as information. The subconscious is a tremendous reservoir of our unrecognised strengths and knowledge. Hypnosis is a natural and effective technique for accessing the subconscious mind and the key to unleashing our <u>potential</u>, so that we can change our unwanted habits and behaviours and find solutions to our problems and concerns. Once the individual has achieved a hypnotic trance state, the hypnotherapist uses many different therapeutic methods ranging from simple suggestions to psychoanalysis. For example, the therapist may ask about past, present or future concerns to establish the reasons for a particular problem. Alternatively, the therapist may give suggestions to the subconscious mind aimed at overcoming specific problems such as lack of self-confidence. While some uses, such as calming a person, need minimal change on the part of the individual, more complex behaviours, such as overeating, panic disorders or depression, require a more complex therapeutic intervention together with psychological <u>homework</u>.

Hypnotherapy is a form of healing subject to much scepticism in the medical and scientific professions, in spite of it being conducted by qualified practitioners. Whilst it has often been clearly ascertained through various studies that a course of hypnotherapy can coincide with the improvement of a patient's medical condition, <u>it is not simple to draw a direct correlation between that improvement and the process of hypnotherapy itself.</u> This is partly because there are few visible or extreme changes to metabolism during hypnotherapy. Further to this, patients react very differently and so a representative sample may not be all that representative at all. This makes it difficult to ascertain who reacts well to hypnotherapy and who just has a natural propensity to recover from the ailment that they were treated for. Many tests have shown that hypnotherapy has helped patients' conditions in conjunction with traditional medicine and that the effect of the hypnosis has only had a purely placebo basis. Patients therefore often have a positive mental response to treatment, but that this is only the patients' perception and is not due to the success of the treatment. Finally, hypnotherapy is often criticised, because those criticising it have little knowledge of the processes and underlying methodology.

Whilst there are doubts about the reliability of hypnotherapy as a method of healing, or, indeed as a method for helping people to deal with stress or to quit smoking, there seems no reason to doubt the effective results that it seems to produce in some patients.

That is the end of section four. You will now have half a minute to check your answers.

(30 second gap)

That is the end of listening test thirteen. In the IELTS test you would now have ten minutes to transfer your answers to the listening answer sheet.

LISTENING TEST 14 TRANSCRIPT

This recording is copyright.

IELTS-Blog.com listening practice tests. Test fourteen. In the IELTS test you hear some recordings and you have to answer questions on them. You have time to read the instructions and questions and check your work. All recordings are played only once. The test is in four sections. Now turn to section one.

Section one. You will hear a conversation between a man and a woman as the woman books her son a place at a summer sports camp.

First you have some time to look at questions one to six.

(20 second gap)

You will see that there is an example. This time only, the conversation relating to this will be played first.

Mrs. Davis   Good morning. My name is Mrs. Davis. I was wondering if this is the place to ask about the summer sports camp?

Philipp   It is, Madam. My name's Philipp and I can answer any questions you might have.

Mrs. Davis   I have a twelve-year-old boy called Dominic and he always gets bored in the summer holidays. I need to keep him busy.

Philipp   We have a group for eleven to thirteen year olds, so that should be fine.

So, thirteen is the correct answer.

Now the full test will begin. You should answer the questions as you listen, as the recording is not played twice. Listen carefully to the conversation and answer questions one to six.

Mrs. Davis   Good morning. My name is Mrs. Davis. I was wondering if this is the place to ask about the summer sports camp?

Philipp   It is, Madam. My name's Philipp and I can answer any questions you might have.

Mrs. Davis   I have a twelve-year-old boy called Dominic and he always gets bored in the summer holidays. I need to keep him busy.

Philipp   We have a group for eleven to <u>thirteen</u> year olds, so that should be fine.

Mrs. Davis   Will Dominic be alright playing with boys a year older than him?

Philipp   Oh yes. We find that at that age group the students haven't usually outgrown each other, so they can play sport together without any problems.

Mrs. Davis   So, who does the coaching of the sports?

Philipp   We are a very professional outfit. The management are all ex-sports professionals and our instructors are usually sports science students.

Mrs. Davis   Are the students on their own with the children?

Philipp   No. They're always supervised by more experienced <u>coaches</u>. Everyone receives an enhanced police check for working with children and we run our own training at the start of the summer. All our staff are ready and trained for groups of children.

Mrs. Davis   What if there are any injuries?

Philipp   All our instructors and coaches are qualified in <u>first aid</u>. There is also the hospital just round the corner if there's a bad injury. It's good to have that nearby, but we haven't had to go there yet.

Mrs. Davis   I know it's unlikely, but it's always possible with that many children running around playing sport.

Philipp   I quite agree.

Mrs. Davis   Now, I want to ask about clothing. I suppose I should make sure Dominic has warm clothing when he goes.

Philipp   Well, Dominic will be there all day and the weather can be changeable. I'd advise you to make sure that Dominic has warm clothing and changes of clothing.

Mrs. Davis   Where will the children go if it rains? Is everything outside?

Philipp   Our location is next to Wentmount School and we can use their <u>sports complex</u> when it rains. It's a big place and as soon as there's any bad weather, we'll be inside.

Mrs. Davis   That's good to know. Now, what parts of the day will Dominic be at the sports camp?

Philipp   We have morning sessions, afternoon sessions or Dominic can stay all day. What would you prefer?

Mrs. Davis   I think all day. He can make lots of new friends and tire himself out. What about lunch?

Philipp   You can send him with a packed lunch or he can join in with the lunches we provide.

Mrs. Davis   What sort of food do you serve?

Philipp   There will be a basic starter such as soup or salad, a solid and hot main course and <u>fruit</u> for desert.

Mrs. Davis   That sounds nice and healthy.

Philipp   Oh yes. It's a sports camp and we feel that healthy food is all part of that.

Mrs. Davis   So, Dominic will only need clothing with him.

Philipp   Well, some sports need special equipment. For example, goalkeepers use gloves and all players use shin pads. I expect Dominic will want to use his own.

Mrs. Davis   Yes, that's true.

Philipp   By the way, as Dominic's a young boy, it would be good for him to have some <u>snacks</u> with him for the mornings and afternoons.

Mrs. Davis   OK. I'll make a note of that. By the way, I don't know the timings of the day. At what time does it all start and end?

Philipp   We start at nine thirty a.m. We don't do it any earlier, as the children are on holiday and it's nice for them to stay in bed a little longer than their normal school days.

Mrs. Davis   That's a good idea. At Dominic's age, children will stay in bed until midday if they get the chance.

Philipp   I've a son that age as well, so I know what you're talking about. The end of the morning session is at twelve thirty and then we start again at one thirty. The afternoon session runs to <u>four thirty</u>. We ask that all children are picked up by five o'clock, as the instructors will need to get home as well.

Before the conversation continues, you have some time to look at questions seven to ten.

(20 second gap)

Now listen carefully and answer questions seven to ten.

Philipp   Now, I need to know some things about Dominic. What games does Dominic like playing?

Mrs. Davis   He likes all sports. He's quite good at cricket and swimming, but <u>his preferred sport is football.</u>

Philipp   OK. We do plenty of all those.

Mrs. Davis   Where do you swim?

Philipp   Wentmount School has both indoor and outdoor pools. We do lots of swimming, both for training and just for fun. It's a great way for the children to get fit and to have a good time. Now, does Dominic have any allergies or anything else we should know about?

Mrs. Davis   He's not allergic to anything. He has strong legs and he can run for ages. He was in hospital sick in December for appendicitis, but that has all cleared up now. <u>One thing is that in the winter, we went skiing and Dominic broke his arm. It's all healed now, but I think that you should be aware of that.</u>

Philipp   Thank you. I've made a note of that. Now, we need to know how Dominic will go home every evening. We have a duty of care to all the children who will be with us and we need to know whether we have to look after them until someone comes or whether they will be going home by themselves.

Mrs. Davis   <u>The first week, I'll pick him up</u> and then after that he can take the bus home. I expect by then he'll have lots of friends to travel with.

Philipp   Good. That will be in Dominic's notes. You can change your plans of course. Just make sure you let us know, so we can make sure he's safe at the end of each day.

Mrs. Davis   I will.

Philipp   Now, the last thing is for you to fill out an application form. You can see the information about all the fees at the end there. Pay the fees by bank transfer and put the reference number in the appropriate box on the application form.

Page 180

| Mrs. Davis | What happens if the course is filled up by the time you get the form? |

Philipp   Don't worry about that. I've reserved Dominic a place. Just call me on the phone number on the form if you change your mind, so I can enrol someone else. <u>I'll keep the place for you for two weeks.</u>

Mrs. Davis   Can I give the form in by hand to you tomorrow? I'll be shopping near here then.

Philipp   That'll be fine. Just make sure the payment is done, as the reservation isn't secure until we receive that. Once we have the form, you'll get an email within a week to confirm everything.

That is the end of section one. You will now have half a minute to check your answers.

(30 second gap)

Now turn to section two.

Section two. You will hear a radio programme with a policeman giving a talk on crime prevention. First you have some time to look at questions eleven to fifteen.

(20 second gap)

Now listen carefully to the information talk and answer questions eleven to fifteen.

Presenter   Hello again, everyone. Welcome back to Radio Coastal. Following the amount of crime we've experienced in the local area recently, we've asked Police Constable Cameron Dawson to join us today and give us some advice on crime prevention. Good morning, Cameron.

Cameron   Good morning, Tracy. Thanks for having me here today. I'd like to give you some advice today on various crime possibilities that you might have the misfortune to experience. To start with, one common theft that the police has to deal with is that of bicycles. Bicycles can be some of the easiest vehicles for thieves and vandals to target and they are easy to sell on to others, making them a relatively attractive source of money. There are various things you can do to safeguard your bicycle, such as locking it securely and doing this in a place where thieves will find it difficult to steal. <u>Another thing that you can do is to take a clear colour picture of your bike and make a written record of its description, including any unique features. Then you can send this to the police, who can get it back to you if it's found.</u>

Another problem in today's society is robbery on the street. While the likelihood of this happening is small, you should be aware of what you can do to keep yourself and your property safe. First of all, if you have to walk alone at night, take extra care. Stay on roads that are well lit and relatively busy. It's important not to carry any important documents, credit cards or excess cash with you and <u>if you think you're being followed, cross the road or go into a shop, tell them your fears</u> and stay there until you're sure you're safe. Don't be afraid of knocking at someone's door in the street either and telling them your worries. Even if they don't let you in, thieves will be discouraged and probably leave the area.

Next I'd like to talk about cars. If you have a car, your vehicle will always be a target for thieves. It can take as little as ten seconds for a thief to steal something from your car, but the good thing is that most vehicle crime is preventable. Make sure you remove everything from your vehicle and don't store

Page 181

anything in the back. <u>A good way to safeguard your car is to develop a regular procedure, so that you take your keys out of the car, close the windows and remove all belongings from it.</u> Follow your procedure and your car will be as safe as it can be.

We've had a rise in the number of cases of identity fraud recently. Thieves may do this in order to buy things in your name and leave you and your bank with the bill and it can be very distressing and difficult to put right. Most cases of identity fraud can be avoided through some simple common sense precautions. First of all, <u>if you've had your bank cards stolen or compromised, make sure you contact your bank immediately to change everything. Sometimes thieves won't take away your wallet, but they'll make a note of the details. This will encourage you not to cancel the cards, but the thieves can buy things online with all the important details in their possession.</u> Another way thieves get hold of your details is when you throw away <u>sensitive material, such as bank statements or receipts. These papers often include information useful to thieves. Stop this by shredding all the papers you think might be sensitive before you throw them away.</u>

You now have some time to look at questions sixteen to twenty.

(20 second gap)

Now listen to the rest of the information talk and answer questions sixteen to twenty.

Cameron   I'd now like to talk a little about cell phone theft, as this has been a problem for a few years now. Having your phone stolen is a hassle. It's not just the handset you lose, it's the numbers, messages and photos too. Cellphone thieves thrive on <u>opportunity</u>, so don't make it easy for them.

Here are some simple things to consider to protect your cell phone from thieves and they're all to do with being aware of your surroundings. First, take care in busy <u>locations</u>, which are popular places for pickpockets, especially if a cell phone is visible in an open bag, or hanging out of a back pocket. Next, think about when you use your cell phone. Outside subway stations can be popular venues for snatch theft, as people instinctively get their cell phones out to check for a <u>signal</u>. Finally, don't leave your cell phone unattended in public places. You wouldn't leave your wallet unattended, but a surprising number of people leave their cell phone on the table while they go to order a drink, or go to the rest room.

Most cell phones have a range of security features that are intended to stop anyone else accessing and using them should they be stolen. One good one is creating a straightforward PIN code that locks your handset. Another PIN feature is that you can set your cell phone to need a separate password or account ID to prevent thieves from simply resetting your cell phone to its factory setting, and therefore resetting any codes or other security features you have set. Finally, many cell phones can be traced, wiped or locked remotely, using another Internet device. These features are useful but will only protect your cell phone if you switch them on. Check the <u>user manual</u> and find out how to do everything.

Knowing how to identify your cell phone if it's stolen is important for getting it back. Each handset manufactured for use has a unique International Mobile Equipment Identity number hardwired into it during the manufacturing process. Knowing this number will help the police identify your cell phone should it be stolen, as they'll need to know more than the <u>brand</u> and colour of your handset. Check the International Mobile Equipment Identity number of your cell phone by checking with its manufacturer's guidelines, which should be available on their website.

That is the end of section two. You will now have half a minute to check your answers.

(30 second gap)

Now turn to section three.

Section three. You will hear two students giving a university presentation to their teacher. First you have some time to look at questions twenty-one to twenty-five.

(20 second gap)

Now listen carefully and answer questions twenty-one to twenty-five.

Professor Black   Good morning. Are we all here? Good. In today's seminar, we're going to hear a presentation from two students. The schedule says it's Lisa and Patrick. Are you both ready?

Lisa   Yes, Professor Black. We're ready. Shall we begin?

Professor Black   Yes please, Lisa.

Lisa   Well, Patrick and I are going to talk about the flower industry in Kenya.

Professor Black   The flower industry in Kenya? I didn't even know they had one there.

Patrick   Oh yes. Kenya's horticultural sector currently ranks as one of the economy's fastest growing industries, the third largest foreign exchange earner after <u>tourism</u> and tea.

Lisa   The industry has been growing every year. The industry rose thirty-one per cent over the last five years with total exports reaching one hundred and thirty thousand tonnes per annum.

Professor Black   How did the industry begin there? It doesn't sound like a traditional Kenyan industry.

Patrick   No. The history of the export of fresh horticultural produce from Kenya dates back to the period before independence when Kenya, then a British colony, was required to help out with the running of the <u>budget</u> for East Africa.

Lisa   After independence the industry continued to thrive with exports starting to go to Europe and thus opening up the potential for Kenya in the export market.

Professor Black   Is Kenya's climate particularly suitable for growing flowers?

Patrick   Yes. Although Kenya is on the equator, considerable differences in altitude allow a great variety of climatic conditions from the hot coastal plain up to the cool highlands. A temperate climate prevails above one thousand five hundred metres, where daytime temperatures are from twenty-two to thirty degrees Celsius and night-time from six to twelve degrees Celsius.

Lisa   Rain days are restricted to sixty to eighty days, so there's excellent radiation most of the year, which is ideal for the year-round growing of quality flowers without the necessity of green house conditions.

Patrick   Kenya has enjoyed economic advantages as well. Kenyan companies have long benefited from favourable <u>exchange rates</u>, making their costs in Kenyan shillings and US dollars relatively low.

Page 183

Lisa   The Kenyans have also set up an excellent logistics infrastructure. Nairobi, the capital city, is a major hub and is very well served by major airlines and charter operators, giving easy airfreight access to European markets and from there to the rest of the world.

Patrick   And labour and energy costs are low compared to other countries. A further advantage for Kenya is that the industry still pays no <u>import duty</u> when sending its flowers to Europe.

Professor Black   How has the industry affected the ordinary people in Kenya?

Lisa   Pretty well. In the agricultural sector, floriculture in Kenya is the second largest foreign exchange earner after tea bringing in more than two hundred and fifty million US dollars per annum. Of course this doesn't all go to the man on the street, but it creates a lot of <u>taxes</u> that contribute to Kenya's public economy.

Patrick   The industry does employ a lot of ordinary people though, with fifty to seventy thousand people directly employed and more than one and half million indirectly employed.

You now have some time to look at questions twenty-six to thirty.

(20 second gap)

Now listen to the rest of the discussion and answer questions twenty-six to thirty.

Professor Black   It seems like an ideal situation for Kenya with no problematic areas.

Lisa   It's not perfect and some years haven't been easy. For example, there have been problems with workforce disputes, which have not yet been wholly resolved.

Patrick   Some years as well have had problems, as high oil prices negatively affected <u>transportation</u> fees. There have also been years when, in spite of the excellent climate, there were heavy rains or extended drought, which negatively affected the size of the crop at those times.

Professor Black   What about competition?

Lisa   Most competition comes from countries that, like Kenya, lie on or near the equator. The four leading global competitors in terms of export value are the Netherlands, Colombia, Ecuador and Ethiopia. These countries compete with each other on the same markets in Europe, Russia, and North America, and competition is getting more tense every year.

Professor Black   What's causing the increase in competition?

Patrick   It's partly due to stagnating demand, but it's also a result of the growing number of large-flowered roses and the generally improving <u>quality</u> of the other countries' products.

Professor Black   Hasn't there been some criticism of the sustainability of the industry?

Lisa   Yes. Although things have improved, wages are significantly below a living wage, leaving workers and their families with limited or no disposable income. Finally, trade union membership is often discouraged and undermined.

Patrick   One of the biggest ongoing criticisms is about water usage. The water footprint of one rose flower is estimated to be seven to thirteen litres. The total virtual water export related to the removal

Page 184

of cut flowers from the area where the flowers have been grown has been colossal. The water leaves the country and the continent and it's not easily replaced.

Lisa   This has caused an observed decline in the levels of local lakes and a deterioration of the lakes' <u>biodiversity</u>.

Patrick   There is also a problem with pollution in the large lakes that supply water for the industry. Initially, everyone blamed the large producers, but it seems that although the commercial farms around the lake have contributed to the decline in the lake level through water abstractions, both the commercial farms and the small holder farms in the upper catchment are responsible for the lake pollution due to nutrient load.

Professor Black   How can this be addressed?

Lisa   There have been calls for sustainable management of the basin through charging <u>water</u> at its full cost and other regulatory measures, but any change in prices has been resisted and there are a variety of political and tribal barriers to getting legislation passed and enforced.

Professor Black   Are there any other downsides to the Kenyan flower industry?

Lisa   Yes. There have been some criticisms of outdated farm methods. However, more farms are increasingly looking into organic methods of <u>pest control</u> and those farms that have implemented water-recycling and waste disposal systems have found that they are able to decrease overall costs in the long run.

That is the end of section three. You will now have half a minute to check your answers.

(30 second gap)

Now turn to section four.

Section four. You will hear a lecture on cotton. First you have some time to look at questions thirty-one to forty.

(50 second gap)

Now listen carefully and answer questions thirty-one to forty.

Hello everyone. Today in this agriculture lecture, we're going to look at the background of one of our most important clothing materials in the United States and that is cotton.

No one knows exactly how old cotton is. Scientists searching caves in Mexico found bits of cotton and pieces of cotton cloth that proved to be at least seven thousand years old. They also found that the cotton itself was much like that grown in America today. The Cotton Belt spans the southern half of the Unites States, from Virginia to California. Cotton is grown in seventeen states and is a major crop in fourteen.

The cotton growing process begins with planting. Planting is accomplished with six, eight, ten or twelve-row precision planters that place the seed at uniform depths and <u>intervals</u>. Young cotton seedlings emerge from the soil within a week or two after planting, depending on the temperature and moisture conditions.

The growing process can be threatened in different ways. Cotton grows slowly in the spring and can be shaded out easily by weeds. If weeds begin to overpower the seedling cotton, drastic reductions in yield can result. Producers employ close cultivation and planters place the cottonseed deep into moist soil, leaving weed seeds in high and dry soil. Herbicides control weeds between the rows.

The cotton plant has evolved with numerous damaging insects, and these insects, if left unattended, would virtually eliminate the harvestable crop in most cotton-producing areas. Plants infested with the leaf-feeding insects are able to counteract somewhat by growing increased numbers of leaves. Many cotton-feeding insects, however, feed on the cotton itself. This reduces the yield and leads to delays in crop development, often into the frost or rainy season. Plant protection chemicals are often used to prevent devastating crop losses by insects. All plant protection methods used on plants in the US are thoroughly evaluated by the Environmental Protection Agency to assure food safety and protection to humans, animals and to the environment. Some plants are also improved by modern biotechnology, which causes the plants to be resistant to certain damaging worms.

The cotton plant's root system is very efficient at seeking moisture and nutrients from the soil. From an economic standpoint, cotton's water use efficiency allows cotton to generate more revenue per gallon of water than any other major field crop. Most of the US cotton acreage is grown only on rain moisture, but a trend towards supplemental irrigation to carry a field through drought has increased in acreage and helped stabilise yields.

Harvesting is one of the final steps in the production of cotton crops. The crop must be harvested before weather can damage or completely ruin its quality and reduce yield. Cotton is harvested by machine in the US, beginning in July in south Texas and in October in more northern areas of the cotton-growing area. Stripper harvesters, used chiefly in Texas and Oklahoma, have rollers or mechanical brushes that remove the whole cotton bud from the plant. In the rest of the cotton producing areas, spindle pickers are used. These cotton pickers pull the cotton from the open buds using revolving barbed spindles that entwine the fiber and release it after it has been separated.

From the field, seed cotton moves to nearby gins for separation of lint and seed. The cotton then goes through dryers to reduce moisture content and then through cleaning equipment to remove foreign matter. Cotton is then moved to a warehouse for storage until it is shipped to a textile mill for use.

Cotton is ready for sale after the quality parameters for each bale have been established. Growers usually sell their cotton to a local buyer or merchant after it has been ginned and baled, but if they decide against immediate sale, they can store. Since it is a non-perishable crop, cotton stored in a government-approved warehouse provides a secure basis for a monetary loan.

An often-overlooked component of the crop is the vast amount of cottonseed that is produced along with the fiber. Cotton is actually two crops, fibre and seed. Annual cottonseed production is about six point five billion tons. This seed is crushed, producing a high-grade salad oil and a rich protein feed for livestock.

One key aspect of this growing process is the management of pests. The most common way of treating pests is by aerial disbursement of pesticides. A crop dusting plane flies low over the crops and sprays the cotton with the pesticides that are in a holding tank under each wing. A careful spraying schedule and pattern should be created and the cotton farmer must therefore have very careful notes on sowing and growing information. The pesticides are squirted straight down from the spray nozzles on the plane. The angle is important. If the spray is sent forwards in the direction of the plane's flight, the droplets will become too fine and be carried away in the wind or in the slipstream of the plane. Some of the pesticides of course will hit the right crop, but some will be untouched. This creates further problems as the farmer will not know which areas are treated and which are not. Re-treating may result in too much pesticide on an already treated area, but not re-treating may affect crop yields. If the spray is sent backwards from the spray nozzles with regards to the direction of the plane's flight, the droplets will be too coarse, which will also create uneven results. A straight down release creates the optimum medium-fine droplet spray.

That is the end of section four. You will now have half a minute to check your answers.

(30 second gap)

That is the end of listening test fourteen. In the IELTS test you would now have ten minutes to transfer your answers to the listening answer sheet.

LISTENING TEST 15 TRANSCRIPT

This recording is copyright.

IELTS-Blog.com listening practice tests. Test fifteen. In the IELTS test you hear some recordings and you have to answer questions on them. You have time to read the instructions and questions and check your work. All recordings are played only once. The test is in four sections. Now turn to section one.

Section one. You will hear a conversation between a man and a woman as the woman interviews the man for a job.

First you have some time to look at questions one to six.

(20 second gap)

You will see that there is an example. This time only, the conversation relating to this will be played first.

Mrs. Allen	Good afternoon. You're Adam, aren't you?
Adam	That's right.
Mrs. Allen	I'm Mrs. Allen. Now, you're here for the cleaner interview here at the hospital.
Adam	Yes.

So, cleaner is the correct answer.

Now the full test will begin. You should answer the questions as you listen, as the recording is not played twice. Listen carefully to the conversation and answer questions one to six.

Mrs. Allen	Good afternoon. You're Adam, aren't you?
Adam	That's right.
Mrs. Allen	I'm Mrs. Allen. Now, you're here for the <u>cleaner</u> interview here at the hospital.
Adam	Yes.
Mrs. Allen	Well, let's get started. I need some personal details from you first.
Adam	OK.
Mrs. Allen	Now, your first name is Adam. What's your surname?
Adam	It's Marshall.
Mrs. Allen	Could you spell that?
Adam	It's <u>M - A - R - S - H - A - L - L</u>.
Mrs. Allen	Thank you. And what is your address?
Adam	It's eighty-two Ackland Road, Gorley.

Page 188

Mrs. Allen	And the postcode for that address?
Adam	It's OG eight, six RE.
Mrs. Allen	Thank you. Next I need your mobile phone number.
Adam	It's oh seven five four three, eight four two, <u>five nine two</u>.
Mrs. Allen	Good. Thanks. What's next? Ah yes. Do you know your national insurance number?
Adam	I do. It's MA six seven, nine five, three six F.
Mrs. Allen	And how old are you?
Adam	I'm <u>twenty-one</u>.
Mrs. Allen	Good. Thank you. Now, you know that this interview is for a part-time job?
Adam	Oh yes. I'm a student at the university, so I wouldn't be able to hold down a full-time job anyway.
Mrs. Allen	So, what kind of hours will you be available?
Adam	My lectures start in the morning at ten, so I'll be available from around six in the morning until nine and then in the afternoons and evenings, starting at around three p.m. I guess I'd want to be free by ten in the evenings. I'd be available <u>mornings</u> at weekends.
Mrs. Allen	Well, we should be able to find you work in those hours. Being a hospital, everything has to be very clean and we need people at all hours of the day and evening.
Adam	That will suit me very well.
Mrs. Allen	By the way, have you had any experience as a cleaner before?
Adam	A little. When I was at school, I did a weekend job at a <u>local restaurant</u>. I did the washing up and helped out with the cleaning. I had to mop down the floors and clean all the surfaces. From time to time, we had to push back all the appliances and cupboards and clean behind everything.
Mrs. Allen	That sounds like good preparation for us. Did you enjoy the work?
Adam	Yes. I liked the people I worked with, so time passed quickly and I made some new friends.
Mrs. Allen	Can we contact them?
Adam	Of course. I asked them when I left if that was alright and the manager gave me his email address.
Mrs. Allen	Do you have that with you?
Adam	Yes. It's david at apple dot com. He said he'd give a <u>reference</u> to anyone who asked.
Mrs. Allen	Good. That will be very helpful.

Before the conversation continues, you have some time to look at questions seven to ten.

(20 second gap)

Now listen carefully and answer questions seven to ten.

Mrs. Allen   Well, Adam. I think we can offer you the job.

Adam   Thanks very much. I look forward to starting.

Mrs. Allen   Now, I'd like to tell you a little about what we expect in the job. You can ask questions at any time.

Adam   OK.

Mrs. Allen   So, to begin with, when you arrive, you need to check in at the <u>staff reception</u>, so your arrival time can be logged in. This will mean that you get paid the right amount. Then, when you finish, you need to log out at the same place.

Adam   OK. I remember that. What is my rate of pay by the way?

Mrs. Allen   You get nine pounds an hour. Is that OK?

Adam   Yes, that's fine.

Mrs. Allen   Now, after you've logged in, you need to go the staff changing rooms. We provide you with green overalls to wear while you're at work, and there is a locker where you can keep your own clothes and valuables safe while you're working. You also need to wear a <u>special hat</u>, which will prevent any hair falling out where it shouldn't. This is especially important if you have to go into the kitchen areas.

Adam   Yes, I had to do that at my last job.

Mrs. Allen   Now, if you work longer than three hours, you're entitled to take a twenty-minute break. During this break, you can do what you want. Some people go and have a cigarette or get some fresh air. We ask you not to go into the public areas during your breaks. There is a <u>staff canteen</u> where you can get free tea, coffee or soft drinks. If you work longer than four hours, then you're entitled to have a meal as well.

Adam   Good. That will save me from some cooking!

Mrs. Allen   Now, we'd like you to start next weekend at nine a.m. Would that be alright?

Adam   Yes, that's fine.

Mrs. Allen   Before you start on that day, it's important that you come for an hour for <u>some training</u>. We need to show you all the equipment and where you'll be working. This will allow you to get on with things straight away when you arrive on Saturday. You'll be paid for this hour of training at your usual rate.

Adam   When shall I come in?

Mrs. Allen   How about Thursday at four p.m.?

Adam   That'll be fine. I'll be here.

Mrs. Allen   Well, that's everything for now. Thanks very much for coming in, Adam. I look forward to you working with us.

Adam   Thank you very much, Mrs. Allen. I look forward to it as well.

That is the end of section one. You will now have half a minute to check your answers.

(30 second gap)

Now turn to section two.

Section two. You will hear a radio programme with a woman giving some people information about a town exhibition. First you have some time to look at questions eleven to sixteen.

(20 second gap)

Now listen carefully to the information talk and answer questions eleven to sixteen.

Presenter   Welcome back to Radio Gem. Now we're going to talk to Mrs. Stephanie French, who is going to tell us a little about the town exhibition that starts next week. Welcome, Steph.

Stephanie   Thank you very much. It's great to be here.

Presenter   So, tell us about the town exhibition, Steph.

Stephanie   Well, as you know, the town has an exhibition every summer. As usual, it will take place in the <u>town park</u> and it'll last from Tuesday the ninth of July until Sunday the fourteenth of July. The exhibition serves several different functions. Firstly, it is a business exhibition, where all local businesses can set up stations, so that people can come and ask them in person about anything related to the businesses. This might range from just general interest to possible business partners setting up new deals. Given our location, the farms in the area have plenty of apple orchards, so there is one particular section on apple juice and other related products.

Another function of the exhibition is to be more like a town fair. There are always games, competitions and amusements to see and take part in. A lot of these things go on throughout the day, but also many of the amusement rides and other things aimed at children open from <u>three</u> p.m. Every evening at ten p.m., the exhibition will end with a big fireworks display, which lasts for twenty minutes. This is always a popular event and the best place to view the fireworks is next to the central lake. Please note that if people plan to take their <u>dogs</u> with them for the evening, be aware the fireworks often distress them. It's often better to just leave them at home rather than giving them stress.

If you're planning on spending time at the exhibition, especially if you're with children, you ought to know that there will be a variety of food on offer. There will be ranges of Italian, Chinese, Turkish, Thai food stations, along with plenty of other international options, and there will also be an open fire barbecue, with meats and <u>vegetables</u> freshly grilled. Naturally, there will be plenty of drinks available as well.

If you're bringing children, make sure that they are suitably dressed. If it's hot, it can be very tiring, especially for young children. Also don't forget to bring plenty of sun screen and a hat to protect their skin. If the weather's bad, don't forget raincoats, umbrellas and think about wearing <u>rubber boots</u>, as the grass areas can get very muddy if there's rain around.

Every day, there are lottery tickets sold and the winning numbers are called out every evening, just before the fireworks. Try your luck and see what you might win. Tickets are only four for a dollar, so you won't need to break the bank. If you can't stay until the evening to hear the results, just write your name and <u>telephone number</u> on the back of the ticket that you leave with the lottery people and they'll call you if you're lucky enough to win.

You now have some time to look at questions seventeen to twenty.

(20 second gap)

Now listen to the rest of the radio programme and answer questions seventeen to twenty.

Stephanie   We've had a number of emails asking for information regarding where things will be found at the exhibition, so I'll talk a little about that next.

As you come in the main entrance on East Avenue, there will be the pavilion with all products to do with apples on your right. This will be an enormous marquee, holding the stations of many of our local businesses. One great advantage of this place is that it's all covered up and a good place to shelter if there's bad weather. They have their own little food and drink section as well, so you can get a hot drink or warm soup if it's cold.

<u>On the left as you enter the exhibition, opposite the Apple Pavilion, as we call it, you'll find the section devoted to all other local businesses.</u> This too is in a big marquee and is an interesting place to wander around and see what is done in our local area. <u>Next to this is the first aid station</u>, which can help you with any minor health problem you have while at the exhibition. They always have three people on duty at any one time and these fully trained first aiders can deal with more serious issues if needed as well as a headache from too much sun.

If you continue down the path away from the entrance, you'll find lots of stalls on both sides with various things to buy. These can include local jams and dried herbs, farm produce, such as eggs and honey, handicrafts in wood and metal, and lots of second hand stalls, where you might be able to pick up a bargain.

These various stalls go right up to the central lake. <u>As you reach the lake, directly opposite will be the area where you'll find all the food stations.</u> There's plenty of outdoor seating with long tables and there are large areas that are covered in case you need to escape the rain or too much sun. The open tables are a great place to watch the fireworks later with an evening drink. It's a popular place, so get there early if you want to find a good spot.

<u>On both sides of the lake, opposite each other, you'll find all the amusement rides and games that can be played.</u> These are areas of great fun both for adults and for children. Make sure that you visit these places at least once with your friends and family. It will be an experience you won't forget!

That is the end of section two. You will now have half a minute to check your answers.

(30 second gap)

Now turn to section three.

Section three. You will hear two students giving a university presentation to their teacher. First you have some time to look at questions twenty-one to twenty-five.

(20 second gap)

Now listen carefully and answer questions twenty-one to twenty-five.

Dr. Williams Good morning everyone. Today, we're listening to a presentation by Toby and Fran. Are you both ready?

Toby   Yes, we are, Dr. Williams. Shall we start?

Dr. Williams Yes please. You go ahead, and as usual I'll come in with various questions as they occur to me.

Fran   OK. So, we're talking about the benefits of electricity as a fuel for vehicles. To begin with, I'd like to talk about energy security here in the United States. Two years ago, the United States brought in from abroad about thirty-three per cent of the petroleum it consumed, and transportation was responsible for nearly seventy-five per cent of total US petroleum consumption. With much of the world's petroleum reserves located in politically volatile countries, the United States is vulnerable to price spikes and supply disruptions.

Dr. Williams But isn't US electricity generated by imported oil as well?

Toby   No. Almost all US electricity is produced from domestic coal, nuclear energy, natural gas, and renewable resources. Using hybrid and plug-in electric vehicles instead of conventional vehicles can help reduce US reliance on imported petroleum and increase energy security.

Dr. Williams Do all electric cars get their power from outside sources or can they generate it themselves?

Fran   They can if they have an onboard generator, but running one will always be more expensive than getting power from the electricity grid. No one would do it unless they have a hybrid car that has an onboard generator and they couldn't find an electricity charging source.

Dr. Williams And do electric cars actually use less fuel?

Fran   Oh yes. Electric vehicles typically use less fuel than similar conventional vehicles, because they employ electric-drive technologies to boost efficiency.

Toby   So, electric cars definitely have lower fuel costs compared to similar conventional vehicles, on the whole due to the low cost of electricity relative to conventional fuel. The fuel economy of electric cars is also highly dependent on the load carried and the slow duty cycle.

Dr. Williams Isn't that true for conventional cars as well?

Toby   Yes, although not so much.

Dr. Williams What other benefits do electric cars have?

Fran   One very topical benefit is of course that they can have significant emissions benefits over conventional vehicles. Wholly electric cars have zero tailpipe emissions, and hybrids produce no tailpipe emissions when in all-electric mode.

Toby   The life cycle emissions of electric cars depend on the sources of electricity used to charge it, which vary by region of the US. In geographic areas that use relatively low-polluting energy sources for electricity production, electric cars typically have a life cycle emissions advantage over similar conventional vehicles running on gasoline or diesel. In regions that depend heavily on conventional fossil fuels for electricity generation, electric cars may not demonstrate a strong life cycle emissions benefit.

Dr. Williams   I've heard that the use of biodiesel in cars is as good in terms of tailpipe emissions as electric cars. Is that true?

Fran   Not really, but there are similar advantages. The fuel B100 reduces tailpipe emissions by more than seventy-five per cent when compared with petroleum diesel, but they're still more than the zero emissions by electric cars. Using B100 biodiesel does reduce greenhouse gas emissions though, because, although the carbon dioxide released from biodiesel combustion is about the same as the fossil fuel engine, it is offset by the carbon dioxide absorbed while growing the soybeans or other feedstock. Tailpipe emissions also depend on which biodiesel is used.

You now have some time to look at questions twenty-six to thirty.

(20 second gap)

Now listen to the rest of the discussion and answer questions twenty-six to thirty.

Dr. Williams   Are there any disadvantages to electric cars?

Toby   Yes. One problem is the current infrastructure availability for refuelling. Public charging stations are not as ubiquitous as gas stations, but charging equipment manufacturers, automakers, utilities, clean cities coalitions, municipalities, and government agencies are establishing a rapidly expanding network of charging infrastructure.

Fran   It's still reasonably flexible though. Since the electric grid can be available almost anywhere people park, electric cars can charge overnight at a residence, a fleet facility, at a workplace, or at public charging stations. Hybrid cars have added flexibility, because they can also refuel with a fossil fuel when there is no electricity charging available.

Dr. Williams   And are the costs of buying an electric car comparable with buying a conventional car?

Toby   Not yet. Purchase prices can be significantly higher. However, prices are likely to decrease as production volumes increase.

Dr. Williams   I suppose that potential buyers know that they can save more money in the long run by using an electric car.

Fran   Yes. That's an aspect that the marketers of electric cars really push hard. I suppose that's natural.

Dr. Williams   What are all the different ways in which people can save money?

Toby   Let's see. The initial costs can be offset by fuel cost savings, a federal tax credit and incentives provided by the relevant state.

Dr. Williams   What about maintenance?

Fran   Electric cars need maintenance just as conventional cars do, but a significant difference is the battery. The advanced batteries in electric vehicles are designed for extended life, but will wear out

Page 194

eventually. Several manufacturers of electric vehicles are offering eight-year or a hundred thousand mile battery <u>warranty</u>.

Dr. Williams   This must be a great perceived drawback to people considering buying an electric car.

Toby   Yes, short-life batteries are a significant disadvantage to electric cars and if the batteries need to be replaced, it can be a significant expense. However, battery prices are expected to decline as <u>technology</u> goes forward and as increasing numbers of batteries are manufactured.

Dr. Williams   Well, that seems to be a good place for a break for you. Do any of the other students have any questions for you?

That is the end of section three. You will now have half a minute to check your answers.

(30 second gap)

Now turn to section four.

Section four. You will hear a lecture on twins and autonomous languages. First you have some time to look at questions thirty-one to forty.

(50 second gap)

Now listen carefully and answer questions thirty-one to forty.

Hello everyone and welcome to this lecture on speech development. Today, we're going to look at twins and how they are theorised to often communicate with each other in their own language.

Twins are regularly reported to invent languages of their own that are unintelligible to others. These languages are known as autonomous languages and, despite current belief, this is not a <u>rare</u> phenomenon. Autonomous languages exist in about forty per cent of all twins, but often disappear soon after their appearance.

So, how does this language formulate? The theory behind a twin language is that siblings are so close to each other and rely on each other so much that they don't have as much of a need to communicate with the outside world, and so they make up their own idiosyncratic language that develops only between the two of them. These siblings actually do not necessarily have to be twins. The typical situation is one in which two or more close siblings grow up closely together during the language acquisition period. If an <u>adult model language </u>is frequently absent, the children use each other as a model and acquire language imperfectly. If a model is completely absent, the children copy other sources, maybe the television or radio, and probably do not create a recognisable language.

In all known cases, any language actually created by close siblings is made up of onomatopoeic expressions, various <u>invented words</u> and words from the adult language adapted to the constrained phonological range of young children. An autonomous language will lack coherent morphology and the word order will be based on pragmatic principles. Because of all this and because the words themselves are hardly recognisable, the language may turn out to be completely unintelligible to speakers of the model language.

A lot of research has gone into autonomous languages. Neither the structure of these autonomous languages nor their emergence can be explained by other than <u>situational factors</u>. Research studies seem

Page 195

to indicate that what appears to be a twin language might actually be two children with the same delay in phonology, which is how children put speech sounds together into words. The delay in phonology is usually due to a lack of models to copy, which are usually parents. Children tend to establish speech sounds in the same general order and they often make identical types of <u>errors</u> in their speech. Children with phonological delays have speech sound systems that don't develop as would be expected, and this makes it hard to understand their speech. Some researchers now believe that what is often described as a twin language is actually two normal children whose speech sounds are not developing as would be expected.

Researchers further theorise that these speech sound errors can be <u>prolonged</u> in twins or close siblings, because each child has a partner who seems to understand him and uses the same type of speech as he does. While this does make their speech a kind of a twin language, as the two children seem to understand each other when others cannot, it's also a delay in sound development that probably needs to be addressed by <u>speech therapy</u>. Not surprisingly, studies have also linked the presence of an autonomous language to language delays in later school age years.

Parents of twins or close siblings who have their own language should not have to panic! There seems to be a small percentage of children who have both their secret language and who are able to communicate effectively with their parents in real language. These children will switch back and forth between their own language and their developing mother tongue, depending on who they're talking to. It's also important to note that researchers have found that not all children who have their own language will go on to have language delays. An autonomous language seems to be only a <u>risk factor</u> that children will struggle with speech and language. However, it will indicate that an evaluation by a speech-language therapist might be beneficial in helping to decide what's really going on.

So, what can a parent do to help their children develop normal speech? Firstly, parents are the most important guide to language acquisition and enrichment. What parents say and how they say it will directly impact their children's development of speech sounds and <u>sentence</u> duration. Therefore, parents should talk to their children as often as possible, describing what they're doing and why they're doing it, what's around them and what's happening. Secondly, it's never too early to start reading to children. Research has indicated that even infants can benefit from this. As all children grow, <u>reading</u> should be a daily part of their routine and it will improve their language, vocabulary, attention and future success. Twins will benefit from this even more.

So, what eventually happens to the autonomous language between twins or close siblings? In most cases, the private language begins to disappear spontaneously, after a low-key intervention, or when the children enter school, interact with other children, and immerse themselves in the more powerful lingua franca. The children might shift to the use of their secret language every once in a while and this is just normal. However, if they are given the right training, they will not develop delay in language learning.

That is the end of section four. You will now have half a minute to check your answers.

(30 second gap)

That is the end of listening test fifteen. In the IELTS test you would now have ten minutes to transfer your answers to the listening answer sheet.

Made in the USA
Lexington, KY
14 January 2019